THE
JOY OF
KNITTING

THE
JOY OF
KNITTING

Texture, Color, Design, and the Global Knitting Circle

BY LISA R. MYERS

RUNNING PRESS
PHILADELPHIA · LONDON

9 8 7 6 5 4 3 2
Digit on the right indicates the number of this printing

Library of Congress Cataloging-in-Publication Number 2001087057

ISBN 0-7624-1060-4

Cover photography by Michael Weiss
Interior illustrations by Dorothy Reinhardt
Technical illustrations by Melissa Allard (p. 98),
Serrin Bodmer (p. 145), and Alicia Freile (pp. 156–160)
Design by Alicia Freile
Edited by Jennifer Worick
Typography: Sabon

This book may be ordered by mail from the publisher.
Please include $2.50 for postage and handling.
But try your bookstore first!

Running Press Book Publishers
125 South Twenty-second Street
Philadelphia, Pennsylvania 19103-4399

Visit us on the web!
www.runningpress.com

In memory of my grandmother,
Eve R. Plotnick

Contents

Acknowledgments

Like knitting itself, writing a book is an activity that may seem solitary but actually takes place within a richly supportive context. I thank Brent Hile, Suzanne Litke, Susan P. Myers, and Martha Onusconich for knitting models of the projects in this book. Charles Loper lent difficult-to-find books about knitting; Nicole Scalessa of the Library Company of Philadelphia assisted with research about Lucy Larcom; Ed Rice translated from the German. Jennifer Worick of Running Press didn't just edit this book; she made it exist in the first place and gave me the opportunity to write it. Jennifer Carpenter helped me carve out time away from our yarn shop in which to write; Suzanne Litke did the same at home. The Knitting Circle at Sophie's Yarns (every Wednesday, 6 to 8 p.m., at the shop) provided constant interest and many of the anecdotes throughout the book. Many thanks to all the knitters of Sophie's Yarns, who surround me every day and are always willing to share their ideas, inspirations, frustrations, and exhilarations.

Chapter 1

Learning to Knit

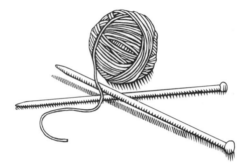

Anew advertising rep calls me at my knitting shop with an idea
for revamping our ad in the local weekly. "I thought maybe a
little sketch of a grandmother in a rocking chair, knitting. . . ."
While she's talking, I look around the roomful of women who have
gathered for our weekly knitting circle. None are grandmothers; only
one is over forty. They are astrologers, attorneys, bankers, computer
programmers, editors, executives, nurses, students, writers. The ad
rep knows that the average age of a reader of her paper is something
like twenty-eight, and she herself (well under that average) knits.

And yet the stereotype persists.

If you're reading this, it is because you knit, or because you'd
like to learn to knit, or you used to knit but think you've forgotten
how (you haven't). First of all, let me encourage you, in case you
have any doubts: knitting is wonderful. It's good for the soul. It can
teach you things about yourself, and about other people—both

those close to you and those on the other side of the world. You can do it anytime, almost anywhere. It can make you deeply happy.

Once, that stereotype of the grandmother in the rocker may have had some validity—but only very briefly. A glance back: for a long time, knitting was a necessity. Socks and stockings were worn—and worn out, constantly—by everyone. Keeping the family's feet covered required endless work by women and girls. After machine-knitted stockings became widely available and affordable (in the early nineteenth century in the United States), there were still hats, scarves, mittens, gloves, shawls, and sweaters. Woolen garments are warm, even when wet, and the elasticity of knitted fabric makes it easy to move in; consequently, knitted clothing makes a good choice for babies and children.

During World War I, men and boys, as well as women and girls, felt they were making a contribution to the war effort from the home front by knitting thousands of socks for soldiers. From the 1920s through the 1940s, the availability of stylish patterns and quality wools gave knitters affordable access to fashion. (Those who remember the Depression and World War II often tell stories of unraveling old garments and re-knitting the yarn into fresher styles when budget constraints or rationing allowed no other wardrobe update.) But then, in America at least, came the Great Change. The unprecedented prosperity of the post-WWII era meant that fewer people needed to economize, and knitting retained unwelcome associations with scarcity and frugality. Developing technologies and the increasing availability of easy-care synthetic fabrics in the '50s and '60s brought a new aesthetic to fashion; handknits began to look old-fashioned exactly because they looked homemade, hand-made.

Most important, women's lives began to change. As more and more women worked outside the home, there was less and less time to knit. In the debates over "Superwoman" and whether it is possible to "have it all," the issues are always career and family. It seems that a leisure activity such as knitting has already fallen by the wayside. So by the 1970s, the cost of a ready-to-wear sweater was already less than the cost of the materials to handknit a comparable one—and that calculation omits the value of the knitter's labor. Today, the retail price of even a handknit sweater may be competitive with the retail cost of the materials. This begs several questions: what are these knitters getting paid? Obviously, someone's making money, but how? And if you can buy it for less, why knit?

I'll return to the first two of those questions in Chapter 11, and the third one shortly. But I think that the stereotype of that grandmotherly knitter must have come into vogue somewhere in the period from the late '50s to the '70s. Many older people continued to knit because they always had, but fewer young ones learned. Those in the middle gave it up after making a few pairs of argyle socks for their boyfriends or, at most, a sweater set for their first baby. A generation gap developed.

And while the knowledge of knitting was never in danger of dying out, it became less accessible. Once, every girl was taught to knit, almost as soon as she was old enough to hold the needles. In some parts of the world, this is still the case. Now, a child who wants to learn may find that Mother doesn't know how (or claims to have forgotten, since she hasn't done it since she was a child herself). Grandma knows, but she lives in Florida. Or a young woman finishes college, gets her career on track, discovers that she has time for a hobby, and asks Mom to teach her. Mom, a lawyer and a card-carrying member of NOW since 1967, marvels that a daughter of hers could be interested in something so . . . domestic, and goes back to editing her brief. Nana is mobile: she is in Wyoming with the Winnebago, completing her tour of America's national parks.

So why do people still knit at all? Because they enjoy feeling creative. Because they can get the sweater they want, in exactly the color they want, with a custom fit. Because it gives them something to do with their hands while they're trying to quit smoking. Because the one-of-a-kind gifts they make for their friends and family express love in every stitch. Because the feel of yarn and needles in the hands is a deep sensual pleasure. Because it calms them and reduces stress. Because it helps to pass the time on the train or bus, and turns an evening in front of the TV into something productive. Because they just saw a dead-plain baby sweater selling for $92 in a boutique and thought, "I can do that!" Because it makes them feel connected to where they come from, and to knitters everywhere.

If the reasons we knit have changed greatly over the past half-century, so have what we knit and the materials we use. Once upon a time, a pattern might call simply for "4 ounces worsted." One would go to the store and choose from eight or twelve or even twenty shades of basic wool yarn. Today one might have a choice of half-a-dozen suitable wools, some of them shinier, some fluffier; some in solid shades, others in heathers, tweeds, or space-dyed multicolors. Let's not even mention the cottons, mohairs, silks, cashmeres, alpacas, and combinations or blends of two or more of the above. Some yarns have metallic strands or glints of Mylar running through them. There are yarns with tiny pompoms or bows or sequins attached to them. Faux fur yarns may knit into fabrics that look like mink, or like something Dr. Seuss might have dreamt up.

Of course, the variety of fibers available changes what we choose to knit. Sweaters and baby blankets are still popular (though the baby blanket may be chenille), but consider some of the other possibilities: cashmere socks, for instance. Sock-knitting is enjoying a renaissance, for excellent reasons; socks make quick, portable projects and luxurious gifts. Pillows are extremely simple to knit and provide a great opportunity for an unusual yarn texture or stitch pattern. Evening bags can be customized to match the dress and shoes, and still be made from start to finish in an evening or two.

Christmas stockings. Dog sweaters. Hats that make your kid look like he has a pineapple on his head. Washcloths. Teddy bears . . . and sweaters for teddy bears, and overalls and dresses and pajamas for teddy bears. Lampshades. Bathing suits. A dust cover for your computer. And yes, a pullover in just the shade of blue to match your new skirt—or your boyfriend's eyes.

If you don't know how to knit, there are instructions and diagrams at the back of this book that can help you begin (see page 156). Let me recommend, however, that you not rely on them. Find a teacher—through a local yarn shop, a night school or adult education program, or by asking around among friends and neighbors. It's an easier and more pleasant way to learn, and it helps keep knitting a social activity rather than a solitary one.

If you already know how to knit: teach someone else. Don't worry that you don't know enough—all you need to know is how to cast on, knit, and purl. Don't worry if you've been told you hold the yarn a strange way, or knit loosely, or if you're left-handed. Teach anyone who wants—or is willing—to learn. There are almost as many ways to knit as there are knitters, and your student can sort out any idiosyncrasies later on. For now, remember the person who taught you to knit, and pass on the gift.

Even if you have never made so much as a scarf, you may once have been taught to knit: many a grandmother has entertained an eight-year-old child on a rainy afternoon with a pair of needles and a ball from the scrap bag. Take a moment to remember how mysterious it all seemed, and how unsure you felt about where to insert the needle as you began each stitch, and how miraculous it was after a few rows, when there was suddenly *fabric* hanging from the needle. Maybe the fabric got wider and wider, maybe it got narrower and narrower, and quite likely it had holes here and there, but it was *knitting*. It was something, where there had been nothing an hour before. This is the miracle of creation; from here, anything is possible.

Before they're old enough to handle needles, many children are given knitting spools (sometimes called knitting knobbies or noddies) to play with. These are hollow wooden spools with nails or hooks driven into one end; yarn is wound around the pegs and then slipped off in a way that produces a tube of knitted fabric. This tube passes through the center of the spool and out the bottom, lengthening into a snake, inches and then yards long as the child gets the hang of the process. Unfortunately, there's not much use for a knitted tube about the thickness of an adult finger, no matter what its length. Some grandmothers can fashion them into doll clothes; some playground supervisors know how to transform them into potholders or trivets. Mostly, however, a child loses interest.

There is an easy way to make that snake with knitting needles, though, and there are reasons why one might want to. Knitters call it i-cord. Some of its uses: to connect a child's mittens to one another; as the tie on a hat, bonnet, or booties; to make loops to go around toggle closures, or knotted as the ball or frog itself; formed into elaborate swirls to embellish a knitted garment. Let me suggest that you take a few minutes to make some i-cord and, since it doesn't take much concentration, spend some time remembering the person who taught you to knit, and your first frustrating, exhilarating knitting experience.

Think about how grateful you are that someone took the time to guide you through your first project and your initial frustration. Think about the wonder you first felt when you finished that simple starter project.

PROJECT:
I-Cord

Materials: You will need two double-pointed needles and some yarn to go with them—any size of either is fine as long as they are compatible. That is, do not choose really thin yarn on really thick needles.

I-Cord:
Cast on 4 sts. Knit them.

Now, the funny part: Instead of turning the needle around, slide the sts to the other end of it. You are still looking at the knit side, though the yarn is hanging off the end of the row that is not at the tip of the needle. Do not worry about it.

Put the point of the empty needle into the first stitch, pick up the yarn, and wrap it around the needle as usual. Knit the stitch. Continue across the row.

Again, when you have knit the 4 sts, slide them to the other end of the needle instead of turning it around. Pull the yarn over to where you need it, and knit across.

In theory, you are making a flat piece of knitting with strands across the back where the yarn is pulled back to the other end of the row. In practice, the fabric will begin to curl into a tube, and the strands seem to get absorbed into it. If you take care to pull firmly as you make the first stitch of each row, the ladder of strands will disappear entirely.

Keep going until your tube is long enough to do something with. You could simply tie it into a bow or knot, and sew it onto the top of a hat. Maybe the cord serves as edging on a throw pillow. Maybe use it to spell out your niece's name and sew it onto her next sweater.

Chapter 2

A Feminist History
of Knitting

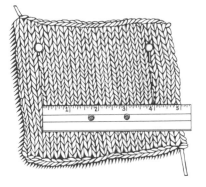

From prehistoric times, knitting, like most other fiber-related activities, has been women's work. Elizabeth Wayland Barber discusses the reasons in her wonderful book, *Women's Work: The First 20,000 Years,* citing an article by Judith Brown: early human societies could only afford to rely on women for those forms of labor which were compatible with childcare, since breastfeeding routinely continued until children were two to three years old. Women's work was whatever could be performed without danger to small children, what could be interrupted and resumed easily and without damage. Thus spinning, weaving, knitting, sewing, and most other tasks connected with clothing were women's work, as well as most aspects of food preparation—but not, for instance, hunting, mining, or smithing.

Even after societies developed beyond the point where survival was full-time work for everyone, the production of clothing was crucial and prohibitively labor-intensive. It takes hours of spinning with a hand-spindle to produce enough thread for a handweaver to use in an hour. Add on hours to prepare the fiber to be spun, hours to prepare the loom to weave, hours to convert the cloth into a garment. For this reason, only the wealthiest people ever owned more than one suit of clothing at a time, and clothes were always patched as necessary until utterly beyond repair. Also for this reason, the work of producing clothing went on continuously, with as little interruption as possible. Girls learned to spin and knit at a young age; until the development of the spinning wheel in the Middle Ages, they used drop spindles that allowed them to spin whether they were watching the flocks, walking, or working at home. Woodcuts from the seventeenth century show this, but the condition persisted well into the Industrial Age: books about traditional fishermen's or Fair Isle sweaters usually include at least one photo of aproned young women knitting outdoors.

Even once the manufacture of cloth had begun to move out of the home, in the United States it remained largely the occupation of women. Young unmarried women filled the textile mills of New England in the nineteenth century, developing their own community. Away from home, the millworkers lived in boardinghouses; they attended classes in subjects like German and mathematics; they produced their own literary magazine, the *Lowell Offering*. Most were sending their wages home to their families on small farms. They were proud of their earning power and enjoyed the sense of independence.

At the same time, they were aware of events in the larger world, and at least some of them considered the broader economic and political circumstances of their employment. In a poem called "Weaving," Lucy Larcom speaks in the voice of a young millworker (which she had in fact been):

"I weave, and weave, the livelong day:
The woof is strong, the warp is good:
I weave, to be my mother's stay;
I weave, to win my daily food:
But ever as I weave," saith she,
"The world of women haunteth me."

Her pride in her work is disturbed by thoughts of slaves in the Southern states where cotton is grown. Their labor fuels the mills as much as hers does, but they receive no wages.

And how much of your wrong is mine,
Dark women slaving at the South?
Of your stolen grapes I quaff the wine;
The bread you starve for fills my mouth:
The beam unwinds, but every thread
With blood of strangled souls is red.

She feels empathy for the slave women, and also guilt because she profits from the system that enslaves them and therefore from their unpaid labor.

These thoughts lead her to a vision of the coming war; she imagines that the cloth she and her coworkers weave will be "shrouds" for "fathers and brothers" who will not wear them because they will die far away on Southern battlefields. The conclusion is no longer in the weaver's own thoughts but rather the poet's voice directed toward her:

But, weary weaver, not to you
Alone was war's stern message brought:
"Woman!" it knelled from heart to heart,
"Thy sister's keeper know thou art!"

The message insists that women workers consider the position of other women in the political as well as the economic sphere. I don't think this is what we expect of the nineteenth-century American woman, particularly one who grew up on a farm with limited formal education. She worked outside the home for real wages, and she considered her own position in the economic system as a whole. She enjoined upon other women a sense of responsibility for, and solidarity with, women everywhere. This was the moment when the Abolitionist movement gave birth to feminism.

Lucy Larcom's contemporary, Emily Dickinson, offers a different perspective. Dickinson lived in town rather than on a farm, and her father's success as a lawyer meant that she didn't have to work outside the home. But there was still household work to be done, and she refers to it in the poem known as "Because I could not stop for death:"

> Because I could not stop for Death –
> He kindly stopped for me –
> The Carriage held but just Ourselves –
> And Immortality.
>
> We slowly drove – He knew no haste
> And I had put away
> My labor and my leisure too,
> For His Civility –

Dickinson has stopped her "labor" in deference to her honored companion, but she has also "put away" her "leisure"—even a woman of Dickinson's class would almost always have had a piece of needlework with her. Ladies who called on one another for tea brought small workbags with them and sewed (or tatted or crocheted) as they socialized. Dickinson's inactivity is a gesture of respect.

It's true that the virtue of such women's needlework had some-what outstripped the necessity; much of what they did was decorative rather than strictly functional. Protestant doctrine—industriousness a virtue, idle hands the Devil's workshop—had replaced real need as the underpinning of habit. The Victorian aesthetic also invited the embellishment of almost any item, no matter how small, so needlework instruction books of the period featured ornamentation for lampshades and antimacassars.

But right beside such patterns are instructions for kneecap covers to warm arthritic joints and many, many utilitarian sock patterns. Perhaps most interesting are the projects explicitly designated as charitable: "This shawl is easy to work and, in a plain yarn, would be suitable for a poor woman." The "poor woman" isn't the reader, choosing garments appropriate to her station. The reader is a lady with leisure beyond the needs of her own family, who gives charity not just in monetary donations but by making things to clothe the poor. (For a twentieth-century glimpse of this practice, see Mrs. Ramsay knitting stockings for the lighthousekeeper's son in Virginia Woolf's *To the Lighthouse*.)

Why doesn't the "poor woman" make her own shawl? Presumably, she can't afford the materials, and/or she doesn't have time because she's trying to feed and clothe her children. Sound familiar? We're catching a glimpse of our contemporary situation, when a handknitted or custom-made garment can be a sign of wealth, not poverty.

Permit me to circle back to Dickinson for a moment. Adrienne Rich, in "Snapshots of a Daughter-in-Law," pictures her "writing [poems] while the jellies boil and scum." This is a moment of anger on Rich's part, that Dickinson's poetry should be forced into what-ever space is left around such, in Rich's estimation, trivial, domestic activities as making jelly.

But in Judith Brown's schema, jelly-making is Dickinson's responsibility because she's a woman, and usually she'd be doing it while taking care of her children rather than writing poetry. Poems thus take the place of children in Dickinson's life. The question is not, "cooking and poems, or poems all day?" but "cooking and poems, or cooking and children and no poems at all?" Rich's unconscious awareness of this is implicit in the very inclusion of the unmarried Dickinson in a poem about a "daughter-in-law" in the first place.

For the last two centuries, knitting in the United States has mostly been part of women's unpaid domestic work, something we did at home to clothe family and friends. It has always been seen as craft rather than art: museums that include embroidered samplers among their exhibits of Americana don't display knitted work alongside them. (Admittedly, this is in part because knitted garments, made for everyday use, have been less likely to survive. But the presence of patchwork quilts in museum collections proves that this is not an insuperable obstacle.) Knitting was mundane, functional, ubiquitous. It's easy to see how it got overlooked, and how feminists of the 1960s and '70s could see it as part of the domestic drudgery they wished to escape. For generations, most women's artistic impulses had been channeled into needlework; during the Women's Liberation movement, we asserted our right to paint or sculpt alongside male artists.

In *To the Lighthouse*, Woolf's heroine, Lily Briscoe, is struggling to be an artist in a society that pressures her to marry and have children instead. Woolf juxtaposes her with Mrs. Ramsay, who has been a traditional wife and mother. Lily paints; Mrs. Ramsay knits stockings. But Mrs. Ramsay is the emotional center of her society and of the novel, as Lily realizes in the second half of the book, when her sense of her own identity is stronger. Then she can see the value of Mrs. Ramsay's "merely domestic" occupations.

Similarly, we who are now secure in our newer roles can now appreciate—and even cultivate—more traditional activities. Thus the traditional distinction between art and craft—that both may be beautiful, but craft produces something which is functional as well—can be seen as giving knitting added value. And to dismiss knitting is to participate in a centuries-old habit of devaluing women's work. So today knitters—both women and men—understand the value of doing something slowly and with care, of going above and beyond the store-bought, the mass-produced. We return to an era of one-of-a-kind and of pride in craftsmanship, and we honor the patience as well as the artistry in our foremothers' work.

If your time is valuable—and whose isn't?—and if your care and effort are valuable, the process for choosing your projects and materials gets more complex, and rightly so. I get angry when I hear knitters say, "Oh, any cheap yarn will do—it's just to keep my hands busy." If we don't respect our work, no one else will. It's been said that the cheapest part of a sweater is the yarn—not just because of the "hidden" costs of a pattern book or the perfect buttons, but because of the knitter's time.

Even if I'm just whipping up a simple baby sweater that will be done in a week, I want to use the best materials I can afford, so that the sweater lasts through several wearers and many washings. I always hope it will be handed down in the family. How much more mean-ingful it is to me when, after spending months on a sweater for my brother, I know he will care for it properly and could wear it for decades (provided I choose a yarn that won't pill easily, and attach the buttons securely). Most of the time, I'm knitting for the long range as well as the immediate future. That does not mean I expect the item to be kept in tissue paper and worn only on special occasions; it just means that I tend to choose styles that I don't think will date easily, I use quality, durable yarns, and I'm careful to darn in the ends securely.

Like most knitters, I feel the lure of the season's hottest color and freshest style, and I've knit mittens in some pretty silly fragile novelty yarns just because they're such a kick to wear. But I don't know any knitter who feels that she has enough time to knit all the things she'd like to, so I think we all ought to choose pretty carefully.

We also have a new model of women's work now: women as executives and entrepreneurs, women with roles as public professionals as well as wives and mothers. Knitting can be part of this life, too, in many ways. One can knit in staff meetings, lectures, and the company cafeteria. Moreover, one can make knitting a business as a shopowner, professional designer, or manufacturer or distributor of yarn. These new career paths don't look much like the older models which involved graduating, marrying, raising kids. Or perhaps a variation on the same theme: a bachelor's degree followed by a master's degree, with marriage and kids juggled while climbing the corporate ladder. The stories I heard when I asked people in "the industry" how they got where they are were usually indirect, even rambling, often shaped by unpredictable outside occurrences and life events more than by deliberate plan. They are perhaps more instructive for all that. We live in a changing world, and we're all still finding our way.

Liza Prior Lucy, co-author with Kaffe Fassett of *Glorious Patchwork* and *Passionate Patchwork* and sales rep for Crystal Palace, Manos del Uruguay, and Rowan and Jaeger yarns, was in graduate school studying psychology when she got a part-time job at a local needlepoint store. Time passed, and she bought into the shop as a partner, then went out on her own to open a new shop with another partner. A few years later, they added knitting. Five years after that, her husband died and the shop lost its lease and closed. With no ties to keep her in one place, she approached her favorite yarn companies and asked about working as a sales rep.

"Female reps were unheard of then [the early 1980s]," she recalls. "I had one male rep tell me, 'You're never gonna make it in this business cause you've gotta tell [the female shop owners] how great they look and how much weight they've lost and how good their haircut is, and they don't want to hear that from you.'"

Along the way, she was designing some sweaters for the yarns she sold; eventually, she submitted a few designs to *Vogue Knitting* magazine and they were accepted. From there she became one of their regular contributors. Her work with Rowan Yarns brought her into contact with Kaffe Fassett, which led to their collaboration on *Glorious Patchwork*, his first foray into the world of quilting. She now lives with her second husband and their two young daughters, and reports on the difficulty of working from home with young children: "People don't understand that sewing is my *work*. It's hard to get used to the idea that you have to leave the laundry and the cleaning [and go into the sewing room] because this is a job." At dress-up time in school, one of her daughters once picked up a briefcase and announced, "I'm a stay-at-home mom and I'm on my way to take the kids to daycare."

Female sales reps are now the rule rather than the exception in the handknitting world. Jan Boyle, a rep for Tahki, Great Adirondack, and Karabella yarns, reports that in 1999 a new company approached her and asked her to represent its products. Far from being put off by her gender or family commitments, the president considered them assets: "He said, 'You're a single mom, you know how to get out there and make things happen.'"

There are women-owned yarn companies and distributorships, and the hand-dyeing of knitting yarn is completely dominated by women: Great Adirondack, Oak Grove, Cherry Tree Hill, Koigu, Schaefer Yarns, Colinette, Lorna's Laces, Prism, Mountain Colors, and Tess's Designer Yarns are all women-owned and operated. The national knitting magazines were, until recently, all edited by women (*Knitters* magazine's promotion of Rick Mondragon breaks an unusual glass ceiling). The design or creative directors at almost all yarn companies seem to be women. Designers are almost exclusively female. Shopowners are overwhelmingly female. Knitting is still women's work, but it's a much bigger world out there than it used to be!

PROJECT:
Möbius Scarf

The idea of the Möbius Scarf is based on the Möbius strip, which is a geometric figure: Cut a long strip of paper. Tape the two ends together, but put a half-twist in one of them before you do. The resulting ring has only one surface—if you draw a line down the center of the paper, you'll go around the loop twice before you meet your starting point, and both sides of the strip will have ink on them.

Why do this for a scarf? Because the twist gives a double thickness of fabric over the wearer's chest, or can be looped over the head to form a cowl; the scarf won't fall off, and thus is harder to lose.

There are several ways to make a Möbius scarf, but I think this is both the most elegant and the most intriguing.

Materials: 5 skeins Mission Falls 1824 wool, or about 400 yds worsted-weight yarn—something soft, cuddly, and not itchy

    40" circular needle size 8, or size to obtain gauge

    ring marker

Gauge: 4 sts = 1" over garter stitch. Note: to test this gauge on a flat swatch, knit every row. The actual scarf is worked in the round, where garter st is k 1 rnd, p 1 rnd.

Scarf:

Cast on 200 sts. Spread the sts out on the ndl in one long flat row; make sure the row isn't twisted around the ndl. Bring the point of the ndl with the last cast-on st around into a loop so it meets the first cast-on st. Instead of inserting the ndl into the stitch, though, insert it into the bottom edge of the cast-on. Then wrap the yarn around the ndl and pull a loop through—this is called "picking up a stitch." Next, insert the ndl into the cast-on edge below the second st and pick up another st.

Continue along the bottom edge, picking up 1 st in every st of the original cast-on row: 200 more sts, 400 altogether. As you go, your ndl will be forced into a double loop—once through the cast-on sts, once through the picked-up sts below them. It may be helpful to put a stopper of some sort on the end of the ndl you're not using, so you do not worry about sts falling off.

When you have 400 sts, the tricky part is over and there's nothing but smooth sailing ahead. Place a ring marker on your ndl after the last picked-up st, take the stopper off the other end of the ndl, and start knitting. When you get back to the marker again, you've completed one round: purl the next one. Continue to work in garter st until the scarf is 9" wide. Bind off.

See what you've done? The bound-off edge is along both edges of the twisted strip; you cast on in the middle and worked out to both sides! Pretty neat, huh?

Chapter 3

Some Facts About Fiber

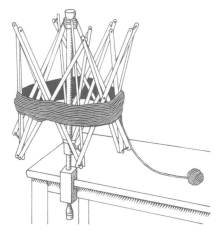

The beginning of knitting as we know it is wool, and the beginning of wool is sheep. Wool from the first domesticated sheep was coarse, not soft and fluffy; E.W. Barber pinpoints the beginning of deliberate breeding of sheep for better and better wool in about 4000 BCE. From wool came yarn, and from yarn comes great joy!

Plenty of non-knitters know the sensual pleasures of woolen sweaters—soft, warm, light, comforting garments. But knitters have these tactile experiences at an earlier stage as well, when we squeeze and stroke the yarn in skein or ball form, and then as it slides through our fingers stitch by stitch.

Other senses get involved, too: the sight of myriad colors and even smell. Yarns can retain the scents of substances used in their preparation: dyestuffs or mordants (the fixatives that keep color bound to fiber), or a eucalyptus rinse to deter moths, or lanolin right from the body of the sheep. These remind us constantly of the yarn's origins as we knit.

Or as we shop. A shop full of yarn is a paradise for eyes and hands, yes, but also for the imagination. Think of the possibilities! Each skein of yarn is a bit of pure potential, and a knitter's mind races as she holds it and contemplates its qualities. The color, perhaps perfect for her son-in-law. The size and shape, bulky for warm outer garments. The texture, soft and silky for a scarf to be worn close to the skin. And that's just one skein. Each different ball or brand will seem to make its own suggestions—"Choose me for that baby gift you need!" "I'm the color you have been looking for to make a hat to match that coat!" "You've used me for afghans before, and now I'm on sale!"

The mind races. It's overwhelming. To own the yarn seems to confer magical powers: all of those possibilities available at any hour of the day or night, should inspiration strike. A supply of yarn in a closet or the basement offers some of the same comforts as a well-stocked larder, without the risk of spoilage. No matter what emergency or crisis presents itself, one will still be able to knit. In the event of nuclear attack, proceed directly to the (well-insulated) basement, and commence knitting socks to keep the family's feet warm through the impending nuclear winter.

Presented with the opportunity to acquire yarn, a knitter may not be entirely rational. While some are disciplined (buying enough yarn for a project and then not buying more until the project's finished), more succumb to the seductions of the sale bin. "There's enough here to make anything I want" becomes as good a reason as "There are only a few skeins left!" Some buy with a specific pattern in mind, others with no fixed idea of what's to come, but all know that the pleasure of owning yarn is a thrill in itself, distinct from the pleasure of knitting it.

Here is my advice as a veteran about how to buy yarn: buy only yarn you like. If you don't like it, don't buy it, even if it's on sale. You won't enjoy knitting with it. Buy yarns you do like when a good opportunity presents itself, whether a sale at your local shop or a visit to a faraway place. (Yarn makes a great souvenir, because it reminds you of the trip throughout the knitting process, and gives you an interesting story to tell about the background of the finished object. And it's easy to cram into a suitcase.)

How much yarn to buy? Consider first its likely uses. A crazy multi-color, multi-texture novelty might make a hat or accent a sweater rather than becoming a whole jacket, and for a hat a couple skeins should be sufficient. If you think you might like a whole sweater, look for ten or more skeins, and check to make sure all are the same dye lot. Don't be surprised if you can't find ten skeins; the yarn may very well be on sale because there isn't enough left for a whole garment. In this case, be stern and honest with yourself: would you really want to wear a sweater with one sleeve made of a different yarn? You may, however, have a project in mind that uses two colors in nearly equal amounts, or you may be thinking of a child's sweater. In either case, go ahead.

Next, consider your purse. There may be twelve skeins left in a perfect-for-a-pullover blue, but if it's cashmere, you should probably plan for mittens, even at the sale price. But if the price is right, be generous in your estimates. Your calculations may show that ten skeins are plenty for a pullover, but if there are twelve in the basket and you can afford them, buy them all: by the time you start to knit it, you may change your mind and want a cardigan. Remember that, if it's on sale, you probably won't be able to get any more of it later. And if you're on vacation in Rome or Amsterdam, that's almost certainly the case.

Finally, take one last look at availability. This may be the kind of novelty yarn that's made for one season and then disappears. Or you've stumbled upon a local craft fair while on a business trip, and these are individually hand-painted skeins being sold by the woman who spun them. These are one-of-a-kind yarns, and this is probably your only chance to buy them. Don't hesitate. Surely there's a little more space in the basement or the closet or the crawlspace or that nook under the stairs.

Which brings me, as buying yarn eventually does, to the problem of storing yarn. A few skeins can be arranged prettily in a basket for excellent decorative effect in the living room, but this is a limited solution. A few bags at the bottom of a closet can lead to a small cedar chest at the foot of the bed, but sooner or later there are likely to be boxes in the basement or the attic. The only real problem with storing yarn in the attic or the basement is the lack of access. You don't just want the pleasure of knowing that you own yarn; you want to be able to use that yarn if the mood strikes—or at least to pick up a ball and swatch it to see if it's right for your next project.

What would ideal yarn storage be like? Everything would be accessible (without a ladder) and everything would be visible. Open shelves are nice and affordable, but balls tend to roll off. Many knitters swear by plastic tubs with snap-on lids (especially good if there's any worry about dampness in that basement), but these can get expensive. Some people develop inventory systems, so they can keep their yarn in boxes but have a complete list of what they have, and in what quantity, and in which box. If you're disciplined enough to maintain such an inventory, this may be the perfect solution for you.

Sorting your yarn collection (sometimes called a "stash") is very important, no matter what system you use. Knitters who do a lot of multi-color work often sort their yarns by color, so they can quickly see if they have the perfect red, or enough yellows for a project in the planning stage. But many knitters—including some who do multi-color work—prefer to keep all yarns of similar weight together, so that they know all the yarns in one spot are compatible with one another. If most of your projects are solid color, you probably want to separate yarns you have in quantity from those that are only a skein or two. You can then tell at a glance from which yarns you can choose for a sweater or other large piece.

Another reason to organize your stash: unless you live alone, your domestic partner/spouse equivalent/kids are going to start looking at you funny when you bring home more yarn if you already have a mysterious jumble of plastic bags spread around. Organized yarn is beautiful, and is much easier to explain as the necessary raw materials of your creative endeavor. If you take your knitting seriously, others will too.

* * *

The "Fiber" in this chapter title isn't just wool. Yarns available to today's knitter can also be made of mohair, alpaca, llama, camel-down, angora, cashmere, cotton, silk, linen, rayon, nylon, acrylic, or dog hair—or any combination thereof. Each type of fiber behaves differently, presenting its own set of advantages and challenges. Even with the best knitting in the world, the wrong fiber can ruin a project. The trick is to know enough about various kinds of fiber to choose the right one for the job. Some fiber characteristics to consider:

Warmth. For most knitting, this is a primary factor. There's not much sense knitting a ski sweater out of cotton. We take for granted that wool is warmer than cotton, but it's important to know that llama, alpaca, and cashmere are all warmer than wool; that linen is at least as cool as cotton; and that silk can seem to behave either way. Synthetics like rayon and acrylic can be confusing: though less warm than animal fibers, they lack the natural fibers' ability to "breathe," and can therefore feel uncomfortably warm to wear.

Elasticity. This matters in the finished garment, of course—no one wants cuffs that stretch out or elbows that sag—but also in the knitting. Wool and wool-like acrylics have excellent elasticity, meaning that they bounce back into shape after being stretched. Cotton, silk, and rayon have little or none. So while the natural "give" of wool makes individual stitches tend to accommodate and adjust to their neighbors, some cotton yarns seem to resist stretching even enough to let the point of the needle in to form the next stitch. This can be an advantage for something like a purse, which should hold its shape despite the weight of its contents. For socks or gloves, on the other hand, which should match the contours of the wearer as closely as possible, choose a yarn with elasticity.

Washability. This is a complex issue. Many people think that wool must be dry-cleaned, but this is not the case; at the same time, some wool yarns are marked "machine washable," some "superwash," some "handwash." What's the difference?

There are two separate issues here. One is water and the other is agitation. The most common fear about washing wool is shrinkage, which requires not just water and agitation but heat as well. There is nothing wrong with getting wool wet; cool water will do wool no harm; if it did, sheep would get smaller when it rains. So why not wash wool in a machine in cold water? Because, even on the washer's "gentle" cycle, there's some agitation, and agitating a wet sweater will stretch it out of shape. If a sweater is small enough— say, a baby sweater—and is put in a net lingerie bag, it should be fine in a cold-water wash; ditto socks, mittens, caps, etc.

Why are some wool yarns marked "superwash?" This refers to one of two processes that treat the fibers to reduce the chance of shrinkage or felting. (See the excellent article in *Knitters Magazine*, Winter 1995, for more about this.) These treatments, however, make no difference in the risk of a garment stretching.

Cotton yarns don't mind water, either (though cotton garments will also stretch if agitated); nor do mohair, alpaca, silk, or most synthetics. Rayon is an exception; most yarns made even partly of rayon will be marked "dry clean only," and they mean it. Linen is another special case: linen garments become softer and more pliable the more they're washed and dried in machines.

Dyeability. Wool, for instance, takes color well—but compare most wool yarns to cotton ones and the cottons will show brighter, stronger, clearer colors. Mohair also produces vivid, intense colors when dyed; combined with the fiber's natural luster, mohair colors often gleam like jewels. Alpaca and angora, by contrast, take dye less willingly; their colors can look pale, soft, subtle, or heathery. This is not to say that these fibers can't be dyed to dark or bright shades, just that those darks or brights may look less so when held next to a similar color of wool or cotton.

Fineness. This has much to do with how soft a yarn feels—the finer (that is, smaller in diameter) each fiber, the softer, silkier, less prickly or itchy the yarn feels. Cashmere, alpaca, and angora are all finer than most wool. But wool itself varies hugely: there are breeds of sheep raised only for meat, whose wool is considered too coarse to be useful, and there are breeds raised for wool, whose wool is still not suited to wear against the skin—though it makes excellent carpets or upholstery fabric. Little or none of this wool ever becomes handknitting yarn. But even within the range of wool types considered suitable for clothing, some are finer than others. Wool from the merino breed of sheep is the finest commercially available and thus commands premium prices.

A caveat: Do not assume that because merino wool is the finest, it is therefore the best to knit with. It is a pleasure to knit and to wear—but like all superfine fibers, it is extremely vulnerable to abrasion. Translation: it pills. In terms of fineness of fibers, the trade-off for softness is durability.

Yarns are often composed of fibers of more than one type, to take advantage of different characteristics in the components. For instance, a yarn that is 80-percent wool and 20-percent mohair will have some of the luster and "fuzz" associated with mohair. The recent emergence of cotton/acrylic-blend yarns responds to knitters' desire for a yarn that is cool in warm weather but has more "memory" than cotton alone. A yarn composed of 10-percent cashmere, 30-percent silk, and 60-percent merino wool will be blissfully soft and springy with beautiful color depth—and without the price tag of pure cashmere or silk. Sock yarns routinely include up to 25-percent nylon because the synthetic gives the wool added strength and durability.

In addition to fiber content, yarns vary in their structure, and this variation makes them look and feel completely different.

First, consider thickness. A very thin yarn makes small stitches and thin fabric; using small needles can produce incredibly delicate shawls or baby sweaters with amazing pattern detail. Pure cashmere and alpaca are often spun into very fine yarns, for two reasons. One, expensive fiber goes further in fine yarn (a finished pullover may weigh 12 or 14 ounces, versus 30 ounces for bulky weight—at what seems like a million dollars a pound, a significant difference!). Two, both cashmere and alpaca are super-warm, and thicker yarns would produce uncomfortably warm garments.

The downside to thin yarns is the amount of time it takes to complete a garment when there are so many itsy-bitsy stitches (all the more if you have fallen prey to one of those beautifully detailed, delicate pattern stitches). Thick yarns use big needles and fewer stitches—consequently, work goes *fast*—after an hour's knitting, progress is clearly visible. With the recent popularity of super-bulky yarns—yarns that work well at 2 stitches to the inch, yarns that need size 15 needles—*Vogue Knitting* has even recommended completing each component of a sweater (the back, a sleeve) in one sitting—and this seems only slightly impractical. (Why do they recommend this? Because slight variations in tension are magnified when stitches are large, so consistency becomes very important.)

Quick-knitting, bulky yarns used to mean thick, warm, cumbersome sweaters. Modern technology has produced yarns that are lighter and softer while still working at large gauges, and knitters' ingenuity continues to develop strategies for working with them. Today's ultra-quick projects are better and more satisfying than ever.

Once upon a time, though, all wool was spun the same way—into thin strands. For thicker yarns, several of the thin strands were then twisted together. The word for this twisting is "plying," and each fine component strand is one "ply," so yarns were designated as two-ply, three-ply, four-ply, etc. Because the original plies were a uniform, standard thickness, all commercially produced "four-ply" yarns were basically the same weight.

In America, they were the kind of thing one would knit on a size 8 needle and expect to get a gauge of about 4½ stitches to the inch. Patterns might call for "3 ounces of two-ply" for a fine-gauge baby sweater, and a knitter might know that she routinely used 58 ounces of four-ply for her favorite afghan pattern. The system was different in different places—English four-ply is that traditional baby weight and twelve-ply from Australia or New Zealand behaves about the same as the old U.S. four-ply. Now that yarns travel all over the globe before they reach the knitter, the old systems chiefly preserve confusion.

Moreover, the "ply" labels to designate weight or thickness no longer necessarily refer to the yarn structure. When I pull a skein each of yarns labeled "four-ply," "eight-ply," and "fourteen-ply" off my shelf, I find that they are actually composed of 4, 3, and 2 strands, respectively. Obviously, the strands in the "four-ply" are each thinner than those in the "fourteen-ply," since the "four-ply" is a skinny little baby yarn for a size 3 needle while the "fourteen-ply" is a big bulky for a size 10, even though it's actually only made up of two strands.

If plies are now spun to be thicker or thinner, why is yarn still plied at all? Why not spin one strand as thick or as thin as we need it? Some manufacturers do, producing single-ply yarns (also called "singles"). But plying improves yarn's strength and durability. A thick yarn made up of thin component plies will pill less than a singles of the same thickness (though again there's a trade-off: the singles will feel softer). Single-ply yarns often have a slightly uneven, handspun look (or maybe a deliberate wildly uneven thick-and-thin look). Plied yarns are more consistent, and they offer many design possibilities: two solid-color strands can be plied with a variegated third, or a wool-alpaca blend can be plied with a slubby (that is, thick-and-thin) cotton. The more complex of these combinations are called "novelty" yarns.

Some of the more common yarn structures are chenille, bouclé, and ribbon (or tape). Chenilles are not actually spun at all: they are very thin strips of woven fabric, cut to produce the characteristic pipe-cleaner-like "fuzz" at each side. Don't be fooled by the lovely drape of the ready-to-wear chenille you've seen; chenille—especially synthetic chenille, as opposed to cotton—is no fun to knit with. You may decide it is worth it, but expect problems. The most common is "worming," in which loops and loose stitches develop as if by magic on the surface of a fabric that was perfectly flat yesterday. "Bouclé" yarns have loops and bubbles of fiber coming out from a central core and are often made of mohair. They make light, lofty knitted fabric that looks thicker than it feels. Knitted tightly, bouclé can look like Persian lamb.

Ribbon and tape yarns are what they sound like: narrow strips of woven or knitted fabric. (They differ from chenille by not being cut: rather, they're woven at the desired width, with finished edges.) These are mostly made of cotton or rayon. Both kinds produce interesting surface textures when knitted. The rayon ones have wonderful luster and drape (as well as a tendency to stretch).

There are other yarn structures—and new ones every day—including chains, felted strands, encased rovings, eyelash. There are yarns with fabric bows sticking out from them, yarns made of paper, yarns with spandex. Plus there are the combinations: why not ply a multi-colored mohair bouclé with a black wool eyelash? A fine mohair with a variegated rayon chenille? Nylon tape with a cotton thread binder?

So after all of this, you're left with the basic question: "What kind of yarn should I use?" Or, "What's the best yarn?" You'll have more luck if you ask a different question, though: not, "Is this yarn good?" but, "Good for what and good for whom?" The best yarn in the world will make you miserable if you're using it the wrong way.

I recommend that you start with instinct alone. Find yarns you like—if possible, yarns you love—and then start thinking about what's appropriate for your project. There are probably types of yarns that attract you automatically (maybe complex ones, maybe smooth or multicolored ones), but no one type of yarn is right for every job. Try to stay open to the pleasures of different yarns and the knitting they invite. Suppose you love to make scarves for yourself out of bright-colored, fuzzy mohair-type yarns. When you find yourself making a scarf for your father, and it has to be plain gray or brown, get a fine, undyed alpaca, and really concentrate on the knitting experience. The quiet softness sliding through your fingers, the subtle heathering in the natural color, may convert you.

You never know.

PROJECT:
Totally Texture Pillow

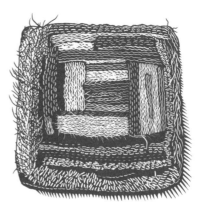

This project should be an adventure in texture and fiber. Gather bits and pieces of as many different kinds of yarn as you can; if you really want to emphasize the variations in texture, choose yarns that are as close as possible to the same color. Don't worry that they aren't all the same weight. Double the really thin ones, and change yarns often: the structure of the knitting itself works to make the yarns accommodate one another.

Finished Dimensions: 16" x 16"

Materials: About 300 yds scrap yarn, averaging worsted- to aran-weight
    circular needles size 8, or size to obtain gauge
    ring marker
    fabric for backing, 17" square
    16" pillow form
    sewing needle and thread

Gauge: 4½ sts = 1" over garter st (i.e. knit every row)

(Note: Exact gauge is not crucial, since you will be working out from the center and can simply continue until the piece is large enough. However, if your actual gauge is significantly tighter than this—say, 5 sts to the inch or more—you may need more yarn.)

Changing Yarns:

As you follow the instructions for "Working the Pillow," change yarns whenever you get bored. Just cut the old yarn and tie it to a new one, leaving about 2" ends of each, and keep going. If you do this on a right-side row, you can weave in the ends as you go and save time in finishing (though since this is going to be sewn into a pillow, no one will ever see if you don't weave the ends in at all; I won't tell if you won't). If you change yarns in the middle of a row rather than at the end, it will keep your edge stitches tidier for picking up later.

Working the Pillow:
Cast on 15 sts. Work in garter st until you have a rectangle that is somewhat longer than it is wide—in this case, about 4". *Bind off all sts, but don't cut yarn. Keep the last loop on the right-hand needle. Rotate the piece a quarter-turn clockwise, so that you're looking at the side edge and that last loop is at the right-hand edge. Now use the same needle to pick up and knit 1 st in each garter-stitch ridge along this edge (i.e. 1 st for every 2 knitted rows). Work back and forth in garter st on these sts until the rectangle becomes square again, and then a bit further, ending with a wrong-side row. (Which is the wrong-side row, since garter st looks the same on both sides? The wrong side is the side where you

can see the ridge from the picked-up row of sts.) Repeat from *, this time picking up 1 st in each ridge and then 1 st in each st of the cast-on row. Continue to work "logs" around the central section, picking up 1 st in every st or 1 st in every ridge. When the piece is 16" long, turn and work your last log only until the rectangle becomes square, then stop. Keeping the last row of sts on the needle, continue to pick up sts around the other 3 sides. Place a marker at the corner, join, and knit in the round for ½" for a seam allowance. (Use a plain or boring yarn here: it's not going to show, and it will be easier to stitch to the fabric.) Bind off all sts.

Finishing:
Block knitting if necessary (it probably won't be). With right sides together, sew knitted piece to backing fabric along three sides, leaving ½" seam allowance. Turn right-side out, insert pillow form, and slip-stitch remaining side closed.

Chapter 4

Knitting in Community

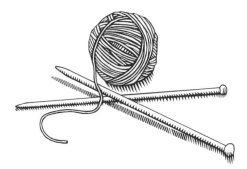

When it comes to working in groups, knitting is a little like reading: you can do it alone—in fact, most of the time, you do—but doing it in a group once in a while makes a pleasant and enriching change.

A knitting group can be you and three coworkers over a table in the office cafeteria (in a Philadelphia law firm, no less!), a formal guild affiliated with a national organization, or anything in between. Belonging to a knitting group reminds you that you aren't the only knitter in your city, which can be an important support some days.

Only other knitters will truly appreciate your trials—the frustration of ripping out inches and inches because of a pattern mistake, the anxiety about running out of yarn before the project is finished. And only other knitters will truly appreciate your achievements—the satisfaction when the sweater fits just right, the pride in knowing that the ripped and re-knit section is now perfect. When your husband says, "Gee, honey, wouldn't it have been a lot less trouble to buy that sweater?," a knitting group will understand why you chose to knit it anyway.

Joining a knitting group almost always makes you a better knitter. Some groups have formal education, with members or guest instructors demonstrating specific techniques at scheduled times. Others don't, but they're still great resources: when you ask a group of knitters about something you do not understand in your pattern, you are likely to learn three new ways to do something. Even when you don't have specific questions, seeing other people's work in progress will show you new strategies and solutions.

And it will inspire you. Things you'd never thought of—or things you'd seen in books or magazines and passed over—will suddenly delight you. A familiar stitch in a new type of yarn will open a new set of possibilities. A better color than the one pictured in the magazine will transform a garment. Someone else's design will give you the answer for a pattern you've been wanting to modify for years. Someone else's cute hat project will provide Christmas gifts for all your nephews.

So how does one join a knitting group? The quickest approach is to consult your local yarn shop. It should have information about local groups, including any coordinated by the store itself. The Knitting Guild of America has local chapters throughout the United States; contact information is at the back of this book (see page 162). If you know other knitters—or if you see someone knitting on a bus or in the park—ask them. Many adult-education programs have knitting classes; contact the instructor and ask her or him.

If you can't find a group, start one. Gather several knitting friends (and tell them to spread the word). Or ask permission to post a notice at your local shop. If your workplace is large enough, look for knitters there via a bulletin board or newsletter. The public library often provides notice space for community activities—and frequently meeting space as well, which you'll need when your group gets going. You can find fellow enthusiasts and meeting space through your church or synagogue. There are more knitters out there than you probably suspect: we're just not very visible. There's a logical corollary to this: If you take your knitting with you wherever you go and make a point of knitting in public places (while waiting for a movie to start, at the hair salon, at your kid's soccer practice), you will attract the attention of other knitters.

Do not feel that you have to be an expert knitter to start a group. You don't have to be any kind of knitter; you are not setting yourself up as a teacher, you are just gathering people to share a common interest. At least at first, probably all you will want to do is sit together and knit and get to know each other: what kinds of knitting each person likes to do, what everyone's current project is.

Eventually, you may want to organize topics for some meetings: several members may be interested in exploring multicolor knitting, or a sweater in the latest issue of *Knitters* may present an intriguing (but difficult to follow) new edging stitch. Or maybe you all have questions about a specific fiber—what is this new Tencel everyone's advertising, and what is it good for? You can devote a session to exploring any knitting topic. If you are sure you need expert advice or instruction, someone in the group may know a knitting teacher who would give a "guest lecture;" otherwise, call your local shop and ask for referrals. But do not assume you need a professional. A group member may know a knitter with lots of experience, or even just a little experience. Someone who's done something once may be a great help to someone who has never done it at all.

Even better, you can often find ways to learn together. If the group is curious about a type of yarn or fiber, invest in a couple of skeins, and try them out: assign one person to make a swatch of a cable pattern, another something lacy, a third something densely knitted like a sock. Make sure to do a couple of swatches in plain stockinette, and ask everyone to wash, block, or otherwise abuse their swatches. When everyone brings their experience to the meeting, even three or four knitters will now know a tremendous amount. Was the yarn pleasant to knit on metal needles or wooden ones? Do small knit/purl patterns show up? Is the ribbing nice and stretchy? Will it stand up to abrasion? Did the machine-washed version get fluffier than the hand-washed? Assign someone to make notes about the results, then photocopy and distribute them to the group at the next meeting. Think how much you could learn in a year if your group meets monthly—even if you only do a "fiber study" every two or three meetings!

Similarly, three knitters together can unravel a baffling set of instructions where one alone is helpless. If not all the members are interested in the new stitch, one might be willing to serve as "reader." The reader is responsible for reading the pattern aloud stitch by stitch while the others do the knitting. This allows the knitters to concentrate on the actual work—it is amazing how much easier it is when you do not have to keep looking up from the needles to find your place in the pattern every few stitches. And it's amazing how many mistakes can be cleared up when several sets of eyes must reach consensus about whether "3 times" refers only to "k2tog" or to everything from the preceding asterisk. You know what I'm talking about.

What else can your knitting group do? Well, it can tell you whether anyone else is ever going to notice the mistake you made 5 inches back that now glares out at you as if outlined in red. It can give you lots of suggestions for what to do when you're pretty sure that you are going to run out of yarn. Rip it out? Add a stripe? Make the sleeves a different color? One of your fellow knitters may even have an odd ball of the right yarn (or something close enough) lurking in her stash at home.

Speaking of her stash at home—a knitting group can hold yarn swaps, in which each person brings what she has at home that she is tired of, has changed her mind about, or otherwise wants to be rid of but cannot bear to throw away. Then it all goes onto a table (the floor, if necessary), and everyone tries to find something she likes better.

A few ground rules may be helpful. Will everyone take back whatever they brought that goes unclaimed, or will it be donated to charity? Should each person take only as much as she brought, or is anyone welcome to as much as she wants? If there is storage available, should leftovers be devoted to a group project for charity like preemie caps or an afghan (see Chapter 12, page 155)?

But what's the difference between a knitting group, and the knitting "community" in this chapter's title? A knitting community does what a group does, and more. If the members of your group have other interests in common, begin to chat about each other's non-knitting lives, or consider knitting in broader contexts (like giving to the needy or teaching schoolchildren), you are on your way to becoming a knitting community.

When you knit "in community," you feel connected in many directions. You feel connected to knitters of the past and to contemporary knitters in other places, all of whose skills and knowledge inform and improve your abilities. You feel an affinity with people who raise animals for fiber, who share your love of fine materials, and whose work contributes to the beauty of yours. You feel a kinship with women and men who quilt or weave or build boats by hand in the belief that the one-of-a-kind and the slowly made are of more value precisely because we live in a world of haste, speed, and mass production.

By way of example, consider Penn Knitters, a group of knitters that meets at the University of Pennsylvania. They gather at lunchtime twice a month; members are kept informed about meeting times and places via a Web page and an e-mail list. The group began when three members of the Internet knitlist (see www.kniton.com/knitlist/index.html) each began to notice that others' e-mail addresses indicated a Penn affiliation. They e-mailed each other and decided to meet. One of them, Bridget Clancy, knew another knitter at Penn—Robin Dougherty. Once this four-some—Bridget and Robin, both librarians, plus Karen Walter (an administrator in the physics department) and Liz Gable (a graduate student)—had met, they went looking for others. They posted notices on Penn "special interest" Web pages and sent a notice to the library newsletter. They had a stroke of luck when the *Philadelphia Inquirer* did a feature story on knitting; several of the knitters mentioned in the article were identified as students or staff at Penn, and Robin looked them up and sent them an e-mail.

As the group grew, one of the most interesting things for its members was to discover how many of them were already acquainted—but always without knowing each other knitted. Ed Rice and Kelly Thomas knew each other from previous jobs, but hadn't seen each other in years when both turned up at a meeting. Beverly Edwards was knitting in the waiting room of the Dermatology Department at the Hospital of the University of Pennsylvania (which is on the campus), because she'd heard at a Penn Knitters meeting that the chairs there were more comfortable than in her department at The Wharton School. One of the nurses saw her and said, "Wait here!" Beverly thought she was in trouble for sure, but it was Joan Lincoln, who disappeared just long enough to return with her colleague, Barbara Sipe, so that both could look at Bev's work. Of course Bev told them about the group. Bridget was

walking on campus one day when she saw someone ahead of her
with a tote bag from a local yarn shop; she followed the knitter
into the hospital complex for some distance before losing track
of her—and finding herself thoroughly lost.

The University of Pennsylvania is Philadelphia's largest employer,
but Penn Knitters bridges many categories (and is one of the very
few campus organizations that do): faculty, students, staff, alumni,
healthcare, business, arts and sciences, library, the Annenberg
School for Communication, administration. At a typical meeting,
people check each other's progress on ongoing projects—Sheila
Dickson's afghan, Royce Hobbs's scarf—and hear about new
ones—Ed is making mittens with cuffs from an outrageously fluffy,
hand-dyed novelty yarn, and several people think they might make
perfect holiday gifts. Mary Jo Pauxtis is wearing a hand-knitted
cardigan that she designed herself and lined (to prevent the bouclé
yarn from shedding on dark blouses). She is repeatedly requested
to take it off so others can examine the lining.

But not all the talk is about knitting. Someone has a handful
of free tickets for a preview of a new Jane Austen movie, which
leads to a discussion of recent movies and also of people's plans
for the evening. Joan took part in a regatta over the weekend, and
everyone is eager to hear about the results. (Sadly, her boat, from
the Philadelphia Girls Rowing Club, was passed by eleven other
boats, while not passing any itself.)

A visitor's presence prompts a discussion of why we knit.
Answers range from the reflective—"It's creative"—to the tongue-
in-cheek—"I always tell people it got me out of prison faster."
Robin started to knit while in graduate school because she saw an
infomercial for the Amazing Sweater Machine and she thought she
could save money (this is greeted by many appreciative chuckles
at her naïveté). Conversation drifts to non-knitters' reactions to

knitting. Beverly says she always tells people, "I go to knitting circle like you go to a bar," because otherwise, "they picture something like a Bible reading—which may also get pretty raucous, but I wouldn't know." Royce relates her new administrator's comment, "Oh, that's so *sweet* that you have your own little knitting group," and adds her own editorial comment on the administrator: "She's [awfully] young."

At the end of the lunch hour, knitters disperse to all parts of the neighborhood. They go back to being nurses, editors, administrators, students, teachers. Maybe the day doesn't seem quite so long. Maybe they feel like more integrated people for having brought their "real lives" into their "work lives."

Maybe we should each be part of a knitting community.

PROJECT:
Collaborative Baby Blanket

Much quicker and easier than the traditional friendship quilt, but an equally wonderful gift. If a member of your knitting group (or any other kind of group, for that matter) is expecting a baby, have each of the other members knit a square, then designate one person to assemble the squares into a blanket. Each knitter can choose her own pattern—a favorite stitch, a motif that represents something about the new mother or child, a pattern she has been wanting to try, or just plain garter stitch in an interesting yarn. Here are some organizational guidelines:

Size and Number: Receiving blankets are often about 24" x 30"; crib afghans might be 36" x 42". Consider how many contributors you have, and how much time. If each knitter makes a 6-inch square,

you will need twenty people for a 24" x 30" blanket (4 rows of five blocks each). It would take forty-eight 4-inch blocks for almost the same size (24" x 32", 6 rows of eight blocks).

Materials: As long as everyone takes care to make each block exactly the right size, yarn weight can vary a bit, but you may want to choose a broad category like "lightweight" or "bulky." Be sure everyone is aware of the washability requirements. Is "machine washable" adequate, or must the yarn go in the dryer as well?

For plain stockinette-stitch squares,
the following are approximate
yardage requirements:

Yardage per Block Size

Gauge	4"	5"	6"
3 sts = 1"	9	14	18
4 sts = 1"	14	20	25
5 sts = 1"	16	24	28

Design:

You can choose a fixed color
scheme—"red and white" or "primaries"—or a general category—
"pastels," for instance—or you can
let everyone do their own thing.
For a really unified look, one buyer
could be appointed to get adequate
quantities of yarn, which would then
be distributed among the knitters.

It may be helpful to request
that every square have a garter-stitch
border—that is, begin and end with,
say, 4 rows of garter, plus have 2
garter stitches along each side—to
facilitate assembly.

Deadlines:

Give everyone as much time as
possible, of course, but make sure the
designated assembler has adequate
time to complete the project. Be
clear about the absolute drop-dead
date for inclusion (and perhaps have
a few fast knitters on deck who
are willing to supply replacement
squares at the last minute for those
who miss the cut-off date).

Chapter 5

Color:
A Little Food for Thought

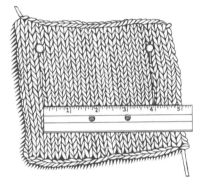

Whether we are looking at a skein or a garment, color is inevitably the first thing that affects us. Shape, pattern, or texture may follow close behind, but our first response is to the color. It's often a profound response, whether we are aware of it or not. Even though we may prefer to think of color as a superficial characteristic, it's not easy to disregard. Having seen the shocking pink blouse on the mannequin first can shape our perception of the garment permanently. We say to each other at the department store rack, "Well, I like it better in blue, but I don't know." After that pink, it's almost impossible to judge the line or cut even in a color we *don't* dislike or find distracting.

Of course, the way we respond to color in clothing is almost never purely visceral, either. It's conditioned by years of training and cultural context. Almost before you can think, "Wow, that's a beautiful color," you're also thinking, "I could never wear that color—it doesn't go well with my complexion/it's too pale for winter/it doesn't match my coat/it'll make me look fat/it reminds me of my grandmother's kitchen/all the magazines say orange is so 'last year'/it will show dirt too easily," and on and on. These are legitimate, practical concerns when shopping for a skirt, but looking at yarn is a little different. You may, first of all, be shopping for someone else, whose color associations are very different from yours. The simple difference in form—skein versus garment—can make it easier to respond to color directly. And your control of the process can make a big difference: the color that you'd reject as too loud in a store-bought sweater may be the perfect cheerful touch in a pair of mittens. If you love a color but are convinced you "can't wear" it, give yourself the pleasure of looking at it for awhile by knitting a gift for someone else with it.

I'm saddened by the number of knitters who drastically restrict their color choices because of ingrained notions about what's "acceptable" on any score. I feel sorry for little boys who'll be dressed in nothing but royal or navy blue from the age of three until fourteen because their mothers and grandmothers worry that deep purple or bright red are "too feminine" (or that their fathers will think so), gray "too mature," goldenrod and ivory "too easy to stain." My heart goes out to knitters who hold a skein of crimson wool lovingly in their hands, while saying "I can't wear red at all." If a yarn comes in three colors you like, by all means, choose the one you think most flattering. But if you love red, you'll look happy whenever you wear that sweater, and that will do more to flatter your face than any beige carefully chosen to complement your skin tone.

When most people think about color in knitting, though, they're thinking of colors—of multicolored hand-dyed yarns and elaborately patterned pictorial sweaters. The variety of multicolored yarns available today is staggering. Some things they all have in common: they allow the knitter to add the visual interest of multiple colors without having to change yarns; they're at their best in simple or plain stitch patterns; and it can be hard to predict the way they'll look "knitted up" from simply looking at a skein or ball.

My first guideline: look for how much light/dark contrast there is among the colors in the yarn, because light/dark contrast trumps all other variations; it is what the eye perceives first. So if a yarn is composed of many deep, moody shades of blue and green, with occasional shots of yellow, the eye will tend to jump to the yellow bits in the knitted fabric—possibly to the exclusion of the many subtle variations in the darker tones. In a hand-dyed yarn, we often find that the bright accent color appears only seldom or in small bits. The dyer has taken the dominance of light/dark contrast into account and restricted it so as not to overwhelm the rest of the colors.

Hand-dyed, hand-painted, space-dyed, and spot-print are all terms that describe yarn with lengths of different colors: red for awhile, then orange, then gold—then unexpectedly lime green—then suddenly red again. If you examine the yarn inch by inch, you'll usually be able to find a repeating sequence that the colors follow. The intervals of each color can be very brief—an inch or even less—or many yards long. There may be one "background" color on which the others appear briefly; this is what is called a "spot print." If the yarn goes from lavender to deep plum and everywhere in between, but never veers off into pink, red, or blue, it may be called "variegated."

These color-change yarns are the ones that drive knitters nuts—both good and bad. They're often ravishingly beautiful in the ball or skein, but it can be maddeningly difficult to predict their effect once knitted—and since they're usually more expensive than simpler, single-colored yarns, mistakes can be frustrating and expensive as well as disappointing. Here are some tips:

Check length of color. An inch of color on a strand of yarn will make a stitch or two in the fabric, so a spot-print yarn will usually produce a swatch that seems to have dots. The more frequently the color changes, however, the more likely the knitting will look mottled or dappled. So if the yarn moves from color to color to color in 1- or 2-inch intervals with no predominating background color, the knitted piece will probably blur to a soft mottled effect (if the colors are closely related to one another) or look densely spotted like a field of wildflowers seen from a distance (if the colors are many and widely varied).

If colors change very slowly—a yard or more of color at a time—expect clear stripes across your garment. If most colors in the yarn continue for 1 to 2 feet, you'll knit a couple dozen stitches before the color changes. This tends to produce a fabric with horizontal streaks. Sometimes, if the color sequence is sufficiently regular, the streaks will tend to line up above one another, producing blotchy areas of near-solid color that might be the size of an egg yolk or the palm of your hand. This is one of the most upsetting results for most knitters.

But cheer up: there are precautions and solutions.

Use two skeins. This is also good for blending non-identical hand-dyed skeins (and are any two hand-dyed skeins ever truly identical?). Knit 2 rows with one skein, then join another skein and knit 2 more. Drop the second skein and pick up the first—no need to cut the yarn. Continue to alternate the two skeins, making "stripes" of 2 rows each. You will not be able to see these stripes in the finished piece, and the technique tends to break up stripes within each skein, as well as blending the two skeins together.

Use two different yarns. Certain stitch patterns—many slip-stitch patterns, for instance—combine two or more different colors in a way that features one yarn, often in "floats" over the surface of another. With a plain background yarn, your multicolor will often show to best advantage, and the mechanics of the yarn changes will disrupt any striping or blotching.

The same is true of Fair Isle patterns: while small-scale, detailed two-color patterns usually get lost in a multicolor yarn, a clear, bold, simple geometric may not.

Do not knit in the usual direction. Most sweaters proceed by casting on at the bottom edge and knitting a rectangle up to the top. But there are alternatives. Try working side-to-side: cast on stitches for a cuff, increase up the sleeve as usual, then cast on many stitches at each end and continue to work *across* the body from one shoulder to the other. Your yarn will still stripe—but now the stripes will be going in the flattering vertical direction, rather than the usual horizontal.

Knit in some *really* unusual directions. Both modular and mitered techniques disrupt yarn color patterns by changing row length and knitting direction. The pillow project at the end of Chapter 3 (See page 42) demonstrates one simple way to do this. For many more, see *Interweave Knits* magazine's Spring '98 issue, *Knitters Magazine's* Spring '00 issue, and any book by Horst Schultz.

Other kinds of multicolored yarns include nepp tweeds, heathers, and marls. If a solid-color base yarn has occasional tiny bits—maybe ⅛-inch long—of different colored wool that are clearly stuck on or spun in, it is usually called a tweed. The spots may all be the same contrast color, or flecks of six or eight or even more colors can dot one solid. These yarns are fairly easy to predict: the spots will speckle the surface of the garment in much the same way they dot the skein.

Yarns called "heathers" are spun of a blend of fibers of two or more colors. The finished yarn often looks subtle or muted in color.

Close examination, however, reveals individual fibers that may be quite different and quite bright. Our eyes do the blending, from red and blue to purple or from green and brown to olive. You can treat heathered (or tweed) yarns as monochrome; their color effects will add a level of subtlety to texture patterns or multicolor designs without obscuring them.

Marled yarns look like candy canes—stripes of two different colors twist around each other throughout the length of the yarn. They are made the way you would think they are: separate strands are plied together to form the finished yarn. Fabric knitted from marled yarns has a salt-and-pepper look that may blur to a mottled or near-solid if the two plies are similar in tone. Very few patterns will read successfully in marled yarns; they're best on plain stockinette or a simple rib.

The two best guidelines I can give for working with multicolor yarns are these: Be patient, and let the yarn tell you what it wants to do. Although some of the effects multi-colored yarns produce only appear over large areas of knitting, making swatches—and ripping them out, and making more—is your only hope of success. Be honest with yourself about the swatches; don't think, "Well, you can see the cable pattern *pretty* well." Instead, think, "Is this the best this beautiful yarn can look?" Try to come to this type of yarn with few preconceptions; don't get carried away as you drive home from the shop planning a certain kind of project in a certain kind of stitch pattern. Stay open and vague: "Mittens . . . something with texture . . . something rustic-looking." Then, rather than being frustrated when the yarn won't cooperate with your plans for it, you'll be able to play with it until the two of you have reached gorgeous common ground.

PROJECT:
Bias-Knit Scarf

Here is an easy way to make a scarf using a technique that brings out the beauty of a hand-dyed or variegated yarn.

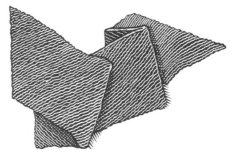

Size: Approx. 8" x 60"

Materials: 2 skeins Mountain Colors ⅘'s, or 400 yards worsted-weight yarn, preferably multi-color
Size 8 needles, or size to obtain gauge

Gauge: 4½ sts = 1" in garter stitch (i.e. knit every row). Note: Exact gauge is not important, since finished scarf size can vary considerably. Experiment until you find a needle size that gives you a nice soft fabric that is not too stiff.

Scarf:
First corner:

Cast on 2 sts. **Row 1:** Inc in each st (4 sts). **Row 2:** Knit. **Row 3:** Inc in first st, k to last st, inc in last st. Repeat rows 2 and 3 until there are 48 sts on the ndl, ending with Row 2. The short sides of the triangle should measure about 8".

Long middle section:

Row 1: Inc in first st, k to last 2 sts, k2tog. **Row 2:** K. Repeat these 2 rows until scarf is 60" along the longest side (that is, the edge that has been increasing continually since the very beginning), ending with Row 2.

See what's happening? You are knitting along a diagonal line across the scarf, so the stripes formed by the yarn are diagonal, too.

Last corner:

Row 1: K2tog, k to last 2 sts, k2tog. **Row 2:** K. Repeat these 2 rows until 2 sts rem. K2tog; fasten off. Weave in ends.

Chapter 6

Working with
Multiple Colors

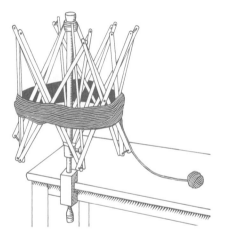

Working with multicolored yarns, as described in the previous
chapter, offers its own delights and challenges, but the
traditional way to get multiple colors into a sweater is by using
several single-color yarns. The subtle shading of Fair Isle sweaters,
the bold snowflakes of Norwegian knits, rich flowers floating
across a summer cardigan, a child's name across the front of his
pullover—all of these are within reach of a knitter who wants them,
with the use of a few simple techniques. This chapter provides an
introduction to those techniques as well as some ideas about how
to choose colors that go well together.

I'd like to spend a moment on some really simple strategies that can produce glorious results, and implore knitters not to overlook them.

First, color blocking: why should the sleeves, front, and back of a sweater all be the same color? Picture a little girl's spring cardigan: the back in lavender, one front pink and one green, one sleeve light blue and one pale yellow. Or a little boy's pullover, the body royal blue, one sleeve bright green and the other stop-sign red. Cute, huh? For an adult, maybe a dramatic, dressy sweater, back and one sleeve black, front and other sleeve white—maybe even white angora embroidered with pearls or sequins. How about a little button-front vest, navy on the back, cranberry on the front, with a little navy watch-pocket? You get the idea.

The next step focuses on horizontal stripes, which are so simple that the how-to can be covered in one sentence. When you get to the spot where you want the color to change, cut the old yarn (leaving a 2- to 3-inch tail) and tie on the new (leaving a similar tail), and continue knitting with the new color. Later, you'll go back and work the ends in on the back of the piece. Some design ideas for these two-color stripes: say your son's school colors are blue and gold; make the body of a sweater blue, and do the sleeves in alternating 1-inch stripes of blue and gold. Running out of yarn? If the second color is perfectly chosen, one striped sleeve on a solid-color garment looks like it was planned from the beginning. Make striped socks, with solid heels and toes on one sock and the same colors reversed on the second.

Stripes don't always have to be of equal width, though. Maybe one sleeve is magenta with narrow stripes of lime, and the other sleeve lime with magenta. Maybe a stocking cap begins with equal stripes of red and white, but the white stripes get narrower and farther apart until they vanish near the point.

What about stripes of more than two colors? Red, yellow, and blue for a little boy's scarf and hat set; light gray, dark gray, and black for a man's. Every shade and texture of purple and blue (with occasional shots of teal perhaps?) in stripes of random width for a dramatic shawl.

Some knitting tips: if all your stripes are even numbers of rows, you'll always join new colors at the same side of the work. If the stripes are less than an inch wide and you're only using two colors, you don't even need to cut and rejoin every time; just carry the unused color up the side of the work (you can twist the two yarns around each other every other row to prevent loose edges). To get an idea of the effect of a particular stripe sequence before beginning to knit, wind yarn around a piece of cardboard in the stripe pattern, letting one wrap equal one row of knitting.

The next level of complexity is bringing a second color into a row of knitting. To do this without actually having to handle two colors at the same time, use slipped stitches. Imagine you've been knitting in blue, but now you cut the yarn and join some white. As you're working the first row, though, you slip some of the stitches—say, every tenth one—from the left needle to the right without knitting them. At the end of the row, most of the stitches on your needle are white, but the slipped ones are still blue. If you continue with white in the next row, you'll have a blue area and a white area with a few blue bits sticking up into it. If instead you go back to blue, you'll have a dotted white line on a blue background.

Or you could change to red next, and slip some of the white stitches. You don't have to work all the slipped stitches on the next row (though if you slip the same stitch for more than two rows, your work may start to get very tight). What if you purl some of the slipped stitches? Play around and see what you like.

Now we come to intarsia. This is the method for most pictures and motifs—a heart in the middle of the front of a sweater, elaborate florals designed by Sasha Kagan, Mickey Mouse. There's only one basic principle to learn here, too: bring the new yarn up from underneath the old yarn so that they interlock. Here's how it works: you are knitting along with ivory and it's time for a purple petal. Pick up the purple yarn, leaving a few inches to work in later, and knit the petal stitches. Pick up another ball of ivory yarn (again leaving a tail) and knit on across the row. On the way back, when you come to the petal stitches, drop the ivory yarn and pick up the purple—from underneath the ivory, so that the ivory yarn is caught against the back of the work by a little strand of purple. When you get across the petal and the background begins again, pick up the other ivory the same way: from *underneath* the purple, so the purple yarn is caught. That's all there is to it. When instructions say to "twist yarns to prevent hole," they mean just this one crossing of new color under old—that is all you need.

When you do intarsia, you're usually working from a pattern chart—you're not just making up the shape of that petal as you go along. The chart looks like a graph, often with symbols to represent the different yarn colors. Charts are worked from bottom to top; each square represents one knitted (or purled) stitch. Usually, knitting begins with the lower right-hand corner; this is the first stitch of the knit row.

The second row is trickier, however: imagine that you've just finished the first row and all your stitches are on the right-hand needle. Now turn the needle around and put it in your left hand to start Row 2. Which stitch are you going to work first? The last stitch from Row 1. Where is this on the chart? At the left edge. So how do you work Row 2? Following the chart for Row 2 *from left to right*. The next row—Row 3—will begin at the right edge again, and so on: odd-numbered rows, knit rows, are read off the chart from right to left; even-numbered rows are purl rows and are worked from the chart reading left to right. You will get used to it.

The other challenge when working intarsia patterns is what I call yarn management. Go back to the hypothetical experiment with the petals: remember joining that second strand of ivory to work the background on the other side of the petal? Intarsia patterns generally require a separate strand for each area of color. If a sweater back has four or five different flowers, each using more than one color, you are looking at well over a dozen strands of yarn hanging from your needle at any given time. Separate balls of yarn for each would be impossible (and wasteful; you probably only need one skein of yellow to do the centers of all the flowers together).

The traditional approach is to use bobbins, small forms (usually plastic now) onto which small quantities of yarn can be wound—akin to spools of thread. Bobbins always have some sort of catch, though, to keep yarn from unwinding until you want it to. If you unwind only a little at a time, the strands don't have any opportunity to tangle.

On the other hand, you spend a lot of time winding bobbins, and they can get pretty heavy hanging off the back of your work. Another approach is to cut strands of yarn, estimating how much will be needed for each small area (one petal, for instance). When that strand runs out, join another. You can comb through the loose strands with your fingers now and then, or just slide an individual thread out of the tangle if you need to. Kaffe Fassett, who is famous for elaborate intarsia designs using forty or more colors in a garment, recommends this technique. It's much less messy than it sounds, and very simple, but if you can't bear the sight of a jumble of yarns on the back of your work-in-progress (though the finished product will be just as neat as with bobbins), this isn't for you.

Not all intarsia designs are irregular, chart-dependent pictorials. Much of Fassett's work is geometric, and this can be a great place to begin. Imagine dividing the back of a sweater into 2-inch-wide vertical stripes, all in different colors—you'd have a strand for each color, and you wouldn't need a chart at all: every row would be the same. Now imagine diagonal stripes: every row has 12 stitches in Color A, then 12 in Color B, etc., but they all move over 1 stitch each time. Easy. Picture squares of different colors in a patchwork effect—again, it's just like vertical stripes, only now all the colors change every 20 rows or so, and Color E replaces Color A, Color C replaces B, etc.

Intarsia isn't hard, just time-consuming. Edna St. Vincent Millay said, "It's not true that life is one damn thing after another [quoting Dorothy Parker]—it's one damn thing over and over." Well, that's intarsia.

There's one more technique for using more than one color in a row. If you wanted to knit a hat with a vine pattern around the border, it would seem silly to start separate strands of green every few stitches—especially since they're all going to link up a few rows later. Instead, you want to carry one strand of green along with the camel-colored background, knitting a few camel stitches, then 1 or 2 green, then a few more camel, then more green, as the pattern requires. This is called *stranded* or *Fair Isle* knitting. It's used whenever the same pattern and background colors are going to persist all the way across a row—a row of hearts, or a name, or an allover snowflake design.

The two challenges with stranded knitting are tension and yarns twisting. When you pick up the green yarn for the next bit of vine after, say, 3 stitches of camel, you can't pull as hard as you would if the 2 green stitches were right next to each other. You have to leave "breathing room" for those 3 camel stitches. There has to be a "float" of green that goes behind the intervening stitches so that they can lie flat. This may very well mean knitting more loosely than you usually do and the knitted fabric may still feel tight when it comes off the needles. Keep practicing, and try blocking your work to even and flatten it out. Give yourself a break, too, and do your first stranded work on a wool or wool-blend yarn rather than a cotton. Wool is much more forgiving.

The problem of yarns twisting is much simpler. Unlike intarsia, it really doesn't matter whether or not you pick up the new color from underneath the old in stranded knitting. But if you're consistent—always picking up from underneath, or always from above—the two strands will begin to twist around each other between the work and the skeins, until they're really difficult to handle. The solution: choose one color to pick up from underneath, and pick up the other from above. It doesn't much matter which is which; people who claim to be able to see a difference usually recommend that the pattern color will be more prominent if it's picked up from below. If you're consistent about doing each color one way, your yarns will never twist or tangle.

If you have large areas of one color or the other—say, more than an inch—it may get difficult to leave the right amount of "float." (You'll also run the risk of the wearer's fingers or shirt buttons catching in those long floats.) The solution is to break up the long jumps by twisting the yarns once past each other somewhere in the middle (or every 3 to 4 stitches if the area is really wide—though if this is the case, maybe the design should be worked by the intarsia method).

* * *

Now you're ready for any kind of multicolor sweater—but perhaps you don't know which colors to use. Here's a basic guide to mixing colors in knitwear.

First, it's helpful to have a way of describing colors. The most common system is to define a color as having three characteristics: hue, value, and intensity. "Hue" is what we usually think of as color itself—a color is red or it's blue; one green has a little more blue in it, the other more yellow. "Value" describes where a color falls on a white-to-black scale—a lavender and a royal purple may have the same proportions of blue and red, but one is much lighter than the other. "Intensity," or saturation, has to do with how gray a color is versus how vivid—one red is bright, another dull.

Practice using these characteristics to describe colors around you, and you'll begin to get some ideas about why certain color schemes work right away. Regardless of whether you were raised to think that blue "goes with" green or not, you'll see that professionals often combine colors that have an element in common. Five soft pastels look good together (same value), or almost any three (or eight!) tropical brights (same intensity), or every type of blue from light to dark and bright to dull (as long as they're all true blues, the same hue). If you usually love blue and purple together, but you're looking at four skeins of yarn that just won't "click," see if one is much brighter or much more muted than the others, and try replacing or omitting it.

A color wheel can also be helpful. The simplest ones have various hues in sequence around a circle; others give shades and tones for each hue, and feature cut-out areas to help you isolate colors or compare the color on the wheel to your yarn, fabric, or paint chip. The wheel will usually have lines on it connecting various hues in relationships that are tried and true.

Many people choose color schemes inspired by nature—autumn leaves, for instance, or the pebbles and shells on a beach. The more closely you learn to observe the natural world—the bark of that tree may have green and gold and ivory as well as gray, brown, and black—the richer your color possibilities will be. Note that natural colors are often much more muted than you think: we say maple leaves are flaming red, but even the most muted skeins of brick and russet may suddenly look garish if held up to the real thing. For this reason, it helps to work from the thing itself rather than a photograph (though if it's April and no fall leaves are available, we do what we must).

Photographs can be great source material, as can postcard reproductions of paintings, as Kaffe Fassett recommends. Paintings especially tend to have unexpected touches of accent color when examined closely, and it's often the color you would never have thought of that brings your composition alive. Try to think of these pictures as training devices, though: they can help you learn to see and combine colors, but using them means substituting someone else's color sense for your own. In the long run, aspire to develop the confidence to strike out in your own direction.

Choosing two colors for a sweater isn't that hard (all of my stripe examples seemed pretty obvious, didn't they?). Choosing three or four colors is a little trickier, but if you stay in the same type of yarn, the colors should all be compatible—color ranges are designed that way deliberately. Begin thinking about proportion: will all colors be used equally in the project, or is one an accent? If the latter, it needs to be different from the others in one or more ways (black among grays, turquoise among sea-greens and -blues, gold among reds).

If you're planning to combine six to twelve colors in one garment, matters reach maximum difficulty: many yarns only come in ten to twelve colors, of which you may dislike a few. Even if the yarn is produced in forty colors, it may only be available in a much narrower range at the local shop. (Give the shop owner a break. Most people are only looking for the one best red, or light and dark gray, not eight blue-greens.) Once you begin to consider using yarns of two or more different types, you add the variables of gauge and fiber content compatibility.

This is the moment to change your thinking and let these challenges enrich the process rather than frustrate you. This is the moment when you cross over into what Kaffe Fassett calls "Glorious Color." It is actually much easier to put twenty or forty yarns together for a garment than eight. If your ten colors don't look right, add ten more and look again. Why does this work? Because the additional colors fill in gaps in the original range. Before, one of the three purples was a little too blue and one was a little too bright. Now, you have six, and they all blend together—you've added another dull one to balance the bright, a slightly plummier one to offset the blue.

When you're gathering yarns for a multi-multicolor project, Kaffe recommends putting them all in a basket and standing back across the room to see the effect. This helps, but it leaves a few questions. First, not every color will necessarily be used equally— try to bury that bright yellow you've chosen for the accent color so it just peeks out between the others, or you will surely think it is too dominant. And will the overall pattern show amid this riot of color? Try separating the yarns so all the background colors are on one side, pattern colors on the other—can you see a clear difference? Bear in mind that the eye sees light/dark contrast first; a pile of "lights" and a pile of "mediums" should be fine together. In fact, they'll be better than a pile of "light lights" with a pile of "dark darks," where the graphic overall pattern is liable to overshadow the subtle play of color within each pile. (For this reason, try to avoid whites and blacks, which pull the eye away from everything else. Instead, choose creamy ivory, pearly gray, charcoal, midnight blue, chocolate brown.)

With knitting like this, you never have to worry about running out of a color; every additional hue, texture, or fiber adds to the beauty and complexity of the whole. On the other hand, you may have trouble finding twenty greens and twenty browns that you like when you're ready to start the project. And not that many projects call for forty skeins of yarn, so you're probably buying more than you need. There's nothing wrong with a little leftover yarn, but the cost sure does add up.

What to do? Plan way ahead, and be patient. Start combing sale bins whenever you see them, putting aside likely-looking skeins until you have maybe half or two-thirds of what you think you'll need. Then take the whole pile with you to your local shop to fill in the rest. (Explain what you're doing when you walk in; maybe even mark your skeins at home so there's no confusion when everything's spread out on the floor.)

You'll probably find that you've bought some duds; don't worry. Save them for next time. Imagine your knitting life as a long and varied process. If you do a lot of multi-multicolor knitting, eventually you will have a complete palette in your stash; then each new project will require a comparatively minor outlay for a few more blues. You'll begin to notice that some types of yarn or color are useful to you again and again; you can buy these on sale even when there's no specific project in the works. It may be helpful to try to stick to one weight category—say, worsted—for awhile to keep your stash a little focused. On the other hand, Kaffe often adds another layer of depth to his pieces by combining strands of two thinner yarns to get a tweedy effect or to match the gauge of the rest of the yarns.

There's no need to worry about matching the gauge of forty yarns exactly; they seem to average out across a garment (provided the colors change often). If you use some form of mitered or modular construction (see Chapter 5) and change directions as you go, the various yarns will pull and push each other into shape.

There's a world of color out there, and never before in history have knitters had such numerous, such vivid, such luxurious color options. Don't be afraid. Dive right in.

PROJECT:
Intarsia Bag

*This easy little bag will give
you a chance to practice your
intarsia skills. (For practice with
fair-isle knitting, try the mittens
in Chapter 11, page 144.)*

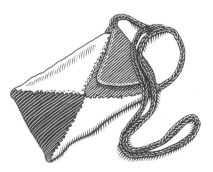

Size: Approx. 6" x 8½"
Materials: Rowan "Cotton Glace,"
one skein each of the following
colors: Pear 780 (A), Ecru 725 (B),
Candy Floss 747 (C), Pepper 796 (D),
or about 50 yds each of 3 colors of
sport-weight cotton and 75 yds of a
fourth color

    Size 4 needles, or size to
        obtain gauge
    2 dpn in same size
    1 small snap
    sewing needle and thread
Gauge: 6 sts and 8 rows = 1" over
stockinette stitch

Bag:
Using Color A, cast on 37 sts. Purl
1 row. **Row 2 (RS):** K1 B, k35 A,
k1 C. **Row 3:** Purl, using the same
colors as Row 2. **Row 4:** K2 B, k33
A, k2 C. **All odd-numbered rows**
from 5 through 35: Purl, using same
colors as previous row. **Row 6:** K3
B, k31 A, k3 C. **Even-numbered
rows from 8 through 34:** Continue
in pattern as established, decreasing
central "A" section by 1 stitch on
each side on every right-side row.
Row 36: K18 B, k1 A, k18 C. Cut
A, leaving 3" tail. **Row 37:** P18 C,
k1 D, p18 B. **Row 38:** K17 B, k3 D,
k17 C. **Odd-numbered rows 39
through 69:** Purl, using same colors
as previous row. **Row 40:** K16 B, k5
D, k16 C. **Even-numbered rows 42
through 68:** Continue in pattern as
established, increasing central "D"
section by 1 stitch on each side on
every right-side row. **Row 70:** K1 B,
k35 D, k1 C. **Row 71:** P1 C, p35 D,
p1 B. **Row 72:** Same as Row 70.
Rows 73 through 141: Repeat rows

in reverse order from Row 69 back through Row 1, thus ending "P37 A." (Cut D when it is replaced by A.) Cut B and C. **Row 142:** Knit. **Row 143:** Slip 1 stitch, p to last st, slip last st. **Row 144:** K2, ssk, k to last 4 sts, k2tog, k2. **Rows 145 through 172:** Rep Rows 143 and 144 (7 sts rem). **Row 173:** Slip 1, p5, slip 1. **Row 174:** K2, slip 1, k2tog, pass slipped st over. **Row 175:** Slip 1, p3, slip 1. **Row 176:** K1, slip 1, k2tog, pass slipped st over, k1. **Row 177:** Slip 1, p2tog, pass slipped st over. Fasten off. **Assembly:** Fold piece along middle of "D" section. Using yarn, sew side seams. Make cord: Using D and dpn, make 48" of i-cord (see Chapter 1, page 17). Using yarn, sew ends of i-cord to top corners of bag. Using needle and thread, sew snap under point of flap.

Chapter 7

Knitting Gifts

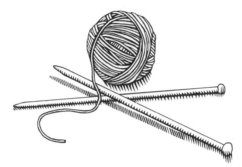

I t *seems* like the simplest thing in the world: You decide to knit
your boyfriend a scarf. He has seen you knitting often enough,
maybe dropped hints about when it will be his turn. His coat is
black, so you find a lovely red tweed, flecked in gray and black. You
swatch several stitch patterns and ultimately settle on a knit/purl
combination that forms a reversible geometric design. Off you go.

As you work, you think often of the moment when you will
present your gift: his surprise, delight, gratitude. The actual event,
however, is nothing like you'd imagined. He dislikes the color ("too
feminine"), the yarn ("too scratchy"), the shape ("too bulky—too
long"). You cannot believe how unappreciative he is of all your
work, how inconsiderate of your feelings, how tactless. There's
a big fight. When the breakup comes a few months later, you
know there were lots of issues—but you keep going back to that
beautiful, rejected scarf.

Welcome to the world of knitting gifts.

It's trickier than it looks, and a bad experience hurts for a long time. There is hope, however: With a little forethought, you can anticipate and avoid the most common pitfalls.

Let's examine the prototypical episode above for hints.

First, a boyfriend: already the stakes are high. Maybe you'd rather knit something for your mother or father—even if she or he doesn't like it, at least the relationship is permanent. You won't later feel that you have wasted time and effort for someone who has disappeared from your life. Still, at least this is a boyfriend of some duration (since he has seen you knitting on more than one occasion). After the third date is *not* the time to decide to knit for someone.

You decided to knit a scarf: good choice! A scarf involves less time and money than a sweater. Most people wear them, even people who never wear hats. And fit is not crucial, as it is with socks or gloves. There is a fair amount of folklore out there about knitting a sweater for your boyfriend, and most of it clearly says, "DON'T." The myth is that you will break up with him if you knit him a sweater before you are married (though some people think being engaged is close enough). The Norwegians have a talismanic solution: If you knit a strand of your own hair into the sweater, it will bind him to you. (I know one woman who, upon hearing this, declared that it explained her husband's attachment to their cat, whose fur is inevitably incorporated into everything she knits.)

Next, that beautiful red tweed yarn: yarn choice is very difficult. Thinking about the color of his coat is good, but also think about everything else he wears. If you have never seen him in red—even some deep burgundy or maroon—there's probably a reason. Maybe this indicates that he only ever wears blue, gray, and black. That's unfortunate, but the time to expand his color boundaries is when you are looking at shirts together at Macy's, *not* when you are putting many precious hours into knitting something, and definitely not when it's a surprise. Most of the time, you want the recipient to like a gift right away, without hesitation or "getting used to the idea." (Note: this caveat applies to the tweed aspect of the yarn as well as its color: though most men will wear a subtly flecked yarn, many will not be comfortable with anything other than a plain solid color. Again, think about what else you've seen him wear, and use that for guidance.)

Consider the texture of the yarn: many tweeds are not very soft. Among all the men I have seen being consulted about yarn preferences for a sweater, the most common concern is softness. It's one issue many women overlook, perhaps because it seems so incongruous next to all that anxiety about whether the color is macho enough. But there it is: The vast majority of men want extremely soft, non-itchy yarns for any garment that will be worn next to the skin (including the sensitive skin of the neck).

Pattern choice: our gift knitter gets lots of credit for experimenting in a swatch before making final design decisions. She gets extra credit for choosing a pattern that is reversible for use on a scarf. But in retrospect, you may wish you had used something simpler. Would the recipient have appreciated its subtleties even without the other problems? Did he even notice?

It may sound like I'm discouraging all effort in making a gift, almost until there's no point knitting one at all. I'm not. But I want knitters to value their time and effort, so that non-knitters will as well. I don't want you to waste time, effort, or money on gifts that won't be appreciated. Therefore, I recommend that you keep a sense of proportion when knitting gifts, and consider what kind of investment is appropriate to a particular occasion and relationship. What you knit for a coworker's baby will, and ought to, differ from what you knit your sister's first child, in materials, style, and complexity.

Here's a story about a really successful knitted gift: once upon a time, many years ago, Mary Helen was with the Peace Corps in Turkey. She had a friend who was also an American Peace Corps volunteer there. When they came back to the U.S., they went their separate ways. He married and lived in New England; she settled in Philadelphia. Time passed. They stayed in touch. He got divorced—and his (now ex) wife threw out all of his artifacts and mementos from Turkey. Mary Helen did what she could to repair the loss (in both respects). She learned to make socks in the Turkish fashion, starting at the toe with a mysterious out-of-nowhere cast-on. She made a pair using eight different colors of wool and subtly different patterns on left and right feet. The first one was finished, the second still on needles when she put them in a box and wrapped them for Christmas, and took the train up to Maine to spend the holiday. He was dazzled. Twenty-five years after Turkey, they picked up where they'd left off.

This illustrates another recurrent theme in the previous analysis: **know your recipient.** I can't stress this too strongly. The more you know about the future wearer—color preferences, allergies, wardrobe staples, leisure activities—the better. Sometimes you must guess with very little to go on, but more often there's plenty of information if you know where to look. Color seems easy; we usually know our friends' and family's likes and dislikes. If that information is not readily available, think about what colors the intended recipient wears most of the time.

Fiber allergies are less obvious. If you don't know any specifics, follow these general guidelines: the softer the better (note that wools treated to be machine washable are often softer against the skin than others). If cotton is suitable for the project, it has the additional advantage of being non-irritating to pretty much everyone. For anything to be worn next to the skin, avoid mohair and angora, unless you know the wearer has no trouble with them.

Consider the **washability** of any potential yarn choice. For a baby gift, machine washability is considered crucial. But this applies to many adults as well. Many women will automatically send sweaters to the dry cleaner, but your brother may throw everything from the hamper into the machine at the Laundromat without a second thought. Do not resign yourself to craft-store synthetics for him, though; the variety of washable natural-fiber yarns available today is staggering. You will still, however, need to impress upon him the absolute prohibition against putting a knitted gift into the *dryer*, and the dire consequences should he forget.

Next, **garment choice.** Try to think about more options than just the traditional sweater, such as a scarf, a hat, mittens, gloves, or socks (if size information is available). You could also knit dishcloths, hand towels, placemats, and tea cozies for unexpected gifts. And what about pillows, afghans, purses, handbags, and totes? As you consider an item, the more questions you can ask yourself, the better. Is this for work or leisure? Is the recipient's taste traditional or contemporary? Does he wear the same things year after year or reinvent a wardrobe every season? Does she prefer patterns or solids? Colors bright, light, or dark? A generous or body-hugging fit? Is the gift intended to be of temporary or long-term use? Will it be enjoyed outside or indoors?

Not all of the questions you ask will have answers, not all will be useful. But one line of inquiry will lead to another, and gradually you will accumulate quite a lot of information. Then you'll find that you approach all the decisions involved with much more confidence.

If you have decided to make a sweater, you may still feel that you're taking a big chance—and you are. This is a case where you may want to forego the thrill of surprise for the security of knowledge. In other words, it may be better to tell the recipient what you're planning. This way you can get input on the tough questions like style and yarn. Try to keep the conversation general, however. Only very experienced knitters with very deep pockets let their nearest and dearest page through pattern books and say, "I like that one." Inevitably the non-knitter chooses something elaborate and/or expensive. If you let yourself get talked into something beyond your skill level or budget, you'll come to resent the project and the recipient. Instead, ask focused questions like, "Would you get more use out of a cardigan or a pullover?" or "Could I make you something to replace your old blue jacket?" or "Which of these two yarns do you like better?"

Whenever possible, avoid making specific commitments, particularly about delivery. Your optimistic target date too easily becomes a looming deadline when someone else is saying, "It's almost my birthday—how's my sweater coming along? It'll be done in time, right?" Better to begin in March or April with something like, "I thought I might make you a sweater for next Fall."

The matter of deadlines brings me to a few words about two more specific kinds of gifts: those for Christmas and those for babies. It's a wonderful thing to think, "This year, I'll *make* everyone's Christmas gifts!" It's an especially wonderful thing to think on the 4th of July. Do not think it on Halloween unless you have a small family and are unemployed. Do not think it on Thanksgiving under any circumstances.

But if it is July, and you're *en route* to the mountains for a couple weeks of vacation, lay your plans. Begin with a list of recipients; decide who's in and who's out this year. (When you see your three great-aunts at Thanksgiving, will you suddenly be overwhelmed with guilt because you planned to buy them fancy soaps again?) Next, decide whether everyone is getting the same thing (a scarf, socks) or whether Dad will get socks, Mom a hat, mittens for the nephews and nieces, etc. Across-the-board gifts

("Scarves for everyone!") can simplify the process without being at all boring. Exploring the endless variations of fiber, color, shape, and pattern can prove as exciting to the knitter as receiving the finished product will be for everyone else. Start making notes about possible colors, sizes, stitch patterns. Consider a knitting journal, useful not just for this project but as a record of all your work. Next year, you'll know whether a hat for your brother should be green or blue to match this year's scarf.

Even if it is New Year's Day, resist the temptation to think "Sweaters! Just for the immediate family, though." Even if your siblings are unmarried and childless, even if you have no grand-parents, this is a formidable amount of knitting. If you decide that you must try it, I recommend that you learn from Mary Brown's example. She knew on January 1 that this was going to be the year, and she hit the ground running. She chose to do Aran sweaters for everyone, which allowed her to buy a very large quantity of natural-white yarn and not waste any partial balls, and also meant that the sweaters had the same general kind of patterning so that all looked good together. (For the record, Mary's "family" in this context meant mother, father, grandmother, grandfather, brother, sister, brother-in-law, and nephew.)

She worked on them all the time—at home, of course, but also on the train to and from work, on outdoor benches during lunch hours, in theaters while waiting for the movie to start. She'd start the back of a sweater and carry it with her everywhere until it became unwieldy. Then she restricted that piece to work at home and began the front as a portable project. By the time the front was too big to carry comfortably, she was usually finished with the back. Then the front would stay home and the sleeves would start traveling hither and yon. She began the back of the next sweater while pieces of the previous one were still at home awaiting completion, and of course blocking and assembly were all done at home (she admits that she tends to procrastinate those last steps, and had something of a finishing backlog toward the end of the year).

Knowing her grandmother wouldn't like (and wouldn't wear) a traditional Aran, she made her a purple shawl. And so that she herself would fit in, she made herself a sweater too. For those of you who are counting, that's six adult sweaters, one child's sweater, and a shawl, within the calendar year: an impressive achievement.

Knitting for babies is another matter altogether. If one is from a knitting family, knitting for new arrivals is automatic, part of welcoming them to the world as well as the household. It seems a requirement: no baby should be without at least one hand-knitted garment as a sign of someone's, or everyone's, care. But the choices and challenges of knitting for infants are quite different from those of knitting even for young children.

First, taste. Since they can't express preferences, how do we choose colors and styles for babies? For color, look to the parents (if the baby isn't born yet); most have either accepted or rejected the traditional pastels in favor of newer brights. If you don't want them to know that you are planning to knit a gift, ask about the nursery furnishings. The answer will also tell you how gender-specific they plan to be (if the baby's sex is known in advance). If the baby is of unknown gender, you still have more options than white, yellow, and mint green: navy blue is nice on everyone, or perhaps royal purple or bright red. Multicolored yarns in a range of bright primaries or rainbow pastels are also wonderful—and they invite the kinds of simple stitches and patterns that knit up quickly.

As mentioned before, **washability** is key for baby things. Many of the synthetics can be tossed in the dryer as well. This is a nice feature in a blanket, but may not matter in a sweater or hat, which will dry quickly on a rack or clothesline. Washable wools are definitely an option, despite many people's hesitations about wool on delicate newborn skin. First, many sweaters do not touch much skin, since they are worn over little shirts or stretch suits. More important, the ultrafine merinos and superwash wools available now are incredibly soft—nothing like the itchy things many knitters remember from our own childhoods. At the yarn shop, hold a skein next to the skin of your neck or inner wrist, and rub it back and forth (the shop owner isn't likely to mind or even be surprised). See how it feels to you. Even better, do the same with a swatch or sample garment if one is available.

Finally, **style and fit.** Fit is much easier than it ever will be again: provided the garment you make has a finished chest circumference more than 16 inches, it will fit every baby at some point. A six-pound newborn may not wear it until the age of six months, while the eight-and-a-half pound newborn may wear it right away, but it will fit sometime during the baby's growth. Bear in mind that parents can always roll the sleeves up, nobody minds if things are a little roomy, and that even in the summer, people are likely to put a sweater on a baby in the evening or in an air-conditioned building. It becomes clear that a lightweight sweater in a 16- to 18-inch size can't fail to be useful.

If you want to make something more specific—a winter bunting, a christening gown—you will face a bigger challenge. Your best bet? Wait until the birth, and see whether the baby is on the large side or the small.

As for style, babies notoriously dislike having things pulled over their heads, so many people prefer to make cardigans. Pullovers with very wide neck openings will work fine, too; look for designs that have buttons at one or both shoulders, placket openings, or boat-neck styles. Beware of older patterns with plackets in the back: now that babies routinely sleep on their backs, buttons can be uncomfortable unless they're very flat.

There's no need to hesitate about a cardigan if you do not know the baby's gender: take the late, great Elizabeth Zimmerman's suggestion, and make buttonholes on *both* sides. Then wait until the baby is born, and sew the buttons on over the superfluous holes. Or, if you plan to give the gift before the birth, put buttonholes on the left front (as appropriate for boys), and rest easy in the knowledge that few people know or care which way is which anymore.

Or dodge the difficulties of fit and fashion by making a hat or blanket. Even the summer baby will use both. Ballpark measurements: a hat with a 15-inch circumference will stretch to cover most newborns through the first six months (go 16 inches if your yarn is inelastic and the infant is 9 pounds or more). Blankets of about 24 x 36 inches fit well in strollers and car seats, while 36 x 40 inches is about right for the crib.

And last of all, a few words in answer to the protest that babies outgrow things too fast for knitting to be worthwhile. First, their things are so small compared to adults' that the projects seem to knit up in no time at all. Second, good work *should* outlast the first wearer so that it can be handed down to siblings or cousins and then put away as an heirloom for the recipient's child. Third, an adorable handmade thing is virtually guaranteed to make you the hit of the baby shower. Finally, it is exactly that disproportion between amount of effort and size of finished product that measures your caring: the difference between what you could have done (by buying some cute little outfit) and what you did (by investing your time and effort in a hand-knitted gift) is the love you feel for that baby and its parents.

And isn't that exactly what you want a gift to show?

PROJECT:
Watch Cap

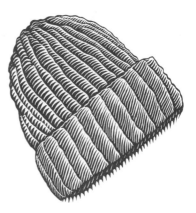

Here's a very basic hat à la On the Waterfront, *made from Manos del Uruguay yarn.*

Size: Adult Medium (but the rib stitch gives it lots of flexibility)
Materials: 2 skeins Manos del Uruguay, or about 175 yards of another bulky-weight yarn
       16" circular needle size 8, or
         size to obtain gauge
       dpn in same size
       ring marker
Gauge: 4 sts = 1" over k2, p2 rib when slightly stretched

Hat:

Using circular needle, cast on 88 sts. Join into a round, being careful not to twist, and place marker to show beginning of round. **Round 1:** (K2, p2) around. Repeat this round until work measures 9".

Shape Top:

When piece gets too tight for circular needle, switch to double-pointed needles. **Decrease Round 1:** Remove marker, k1, replace marker; (k1, p2, k2, p1, k2tog) 11 times around. (77 sts) **Round 2:** (K1, p2, k2, p1, k1) around. **Round 3:** (K1, p2, k2, k2tog) around. (66 sts) **Round 4:** (K1, p2, k3) around. **Round 5:** (K1, p2, k1, k2tog) around. (55 sts) **Round 6:** (K1, p2, k2) around. **Round 7:** (K1, p2, k2tog) around. (44 sts) **Round 8:** (K1, p2, k1) around. **Round 9:** (K1, p1, k2tog) around. (33 sts) **Round 10:** (K1, p1, k1) around. **Round 11:** (K1, k2tog) around. (22 sts) **Round 12:** Knit. **Round 13:** K2tog around. (11 sts) Cut yarn; thread through remaining sts; fasten off. Weave in ends.

Chapter 8

Texture

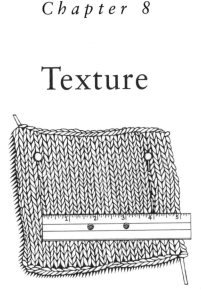

E ver heard of the "knitter's handshake?" Someone approaches
you, hand outstretched, but reaches for your sleeve instead of
your hand—she or he wants to touch your sweater! It is almost
unconscious at fiber-related events. After all, we're all constantly
touching everything that's on display or for sale, and some of the
most wonderful things are on the other knitters. You may feel
someone stroking your shoulder, and turn to find a stranger. Most
people quickly grow accustomed to the experience. In fact, most
people quickly engage in conversation with the other knitter.
What yarn is this? Did you make up the pattern yourself? Do I
recognize the stitch?

We're a sociable bunch.

Knitting is a very visual activity, yes, but it's also extremely
tactile. You see the sweater and you want to touch it. If you saw
wallpaper in the same beautiful shade, you wouldn't feel drawn to

touch. The tactile pleasure comes from the yarn itself, and also from the knitting. The fabric can be smooth or pebbly, sculpted or thick and cushy, all depending on the knitted stitch.

Here are two experiments to try with texture. The first is one you think you already understand: get three yarns—one plain, one something like a chenille, and one a fuzzy mohair. Now knit the same swatch with each one: Cast on 20 sts. Row 1: K6, p2, k4, p2, k6. Rows 2 and 4: P6, k2, p4, k2, p6. Row 3: K6, p2, slip next 2 sts onto a cable needle and hold at back of work, k2, k2 from cable needle, p2, k6. Repeat these 4 rows four times, then repeat Rows 1 and 2 once more and bind off.

Compare the swatches. The pattern is probably clearest on the plain yarn, but you can certainly see the cable on the other two as well. Working the cable twist on Row 3 may have been difficult with the chenille yarn, which probably didn't stretch easily. The two purl stitches on either side of the cable probably show more clearly on the mohair than on the plain yarn, where they tend to scrunch together. They may even look too big or too loose on the chenille. It is easy to imagine bigger cables looking even better on the fuzzy-textured yarns. This is a general rule: the heavier or more highly textured the yarn, the bolder the pattern has to be in order to be effective.

Now try the second experiment. Using just the plain yarn, knit the following swatch: Cast on 19 sts. Rows 1–12: (K1, p1) across, ending k1. Row 13: K1, p1, k15, p1, k1. Row 14: K1, p1, k1, p13, k1, p1, k1. Repeat Rows 13 and 14 five more times. Bind off. Knit two more swatches just like this one, still using the plain yarn, but for one swatch use needles two sizes smaller than you did at first, and for the other use needles two sizes larger.

The differences among the three swatches are harder to see than in the first experiment, but they're more profound. The swatch with the smallest needle may look tight, and the one with the largest will probably look loose. Look more closely at the stitches in the top, plain part of the swatch: the tighter knitting probably looks more regular and even than the looser. The bottom area of the swatch, the seed stitch part, may be more clearly defined in the tighter swatches, or it may shrink down to a subtle pebbly surface without distinct stitches at all.

Close your eyes and feel all three swatches. If you squeeze them, the looser ones should feel softer. If you tug them in different directions, the tight swatch will probably offer more resistance—though the loosest swatch may feel like it is not going to bounce back into the original shape. If you hang all three over your wrist, the loose one should flop easily, while the tight one may not drape at all.

So which needle size should you use with this yarn? It's a trick question. The answer is: What are you trying to make? For a scarf or shawl, you want maximum softness and drape, so you would use a larger needle. For a purse, you want something dense and durable that holds its shape, so you would use a smaller needle. For a sweater, you want comfortable ease but good "memory," so you might use the middle size (or you might opt for a needle one size smaller if you like the clarity of the pattern stitch better, etc.). How did you decide which needle to use first, the medium-sized needle? If you followed the recommendation on the yarn label, you should have a medium-density fabric suitable for a sweater; most yarns are labeled with sweater-knitting in mind.

We can learn even more from these swatches. Measure the gauge of each one—that is, use a ruler or tape measure to figure out how many stitches fit in 1 inch. The numbers may be very different—6 stitches in an inch on the tight swatch, 4 on the loose—or they may be closer together. But you've seen (and felt) how different the swatches are. If a pattern were to call for a yarn that knits at 4 stitches to the inch, your yarn would do it—but it would look very loose. It is possible to knit almost any yarn at lots of different gauges; the question is not, "Will this yarn get 4 stitches to an inch?" but rather, "Do I like it at that gauge?" "Does the pattern show well enough?" "Is the fabric still soft enough?" "Do my fingers ache if I knit tightly enough for this gauge?"

Gauge is a very personal thing. Some knitters hold needles and yarn very tightly; some seem to let them float by themselves. This is why patterns always say things like, "Size 8 needles—OR SIZE TO OBTAIN GAUGE." The needle size you wind up using is not important; the *gauge* is. One knitter may need to use a size 9 needle for that gauge, another may go all the way down to a 3—for the same yarn. The knitter who uses a size 7 for that yarn may need to go to a 6 or 8 for the same gauge on a different stitch pattern. Knowing that you tend to knit more tightly than average will save you time in making your gauge swatch, because you can start with a larger needle than the one specified.

Notice I didn't say that knowing you're a tight knitter can save you time by letting you skip the gauge swatch. Skipping the gauge swatch will *never* save you time.

Stop!

I'm so serious about this that I want to be careful not to exaggerate. Skipping the gauge swatch may save time on about 2 to 4 percent of your projects: the ones where you are using a yarn you have worked with before, in a stitch pattern you have knitted before, *and* with the same size needles you used last time (if you can remember what that was).

Will skipping the swatch cost you extra time in the other 96 percent of projects? No, only in a quarter to a third of them—those are the ones where you start knitting, realize that you are using the wrong-size needle, and have to rip out and start again. As you can imagine, this is very frustrating. The rest of the time, the results will not be far enough off for you to bother starting again, but they will not be perfect, either. The garment will be coming out a little larger or smaller than you intended, or the fabric will be a little softer or a little denser, and you'll decide that it's "close enough," and not worth ripping out.

There's nothing wrong with working this way, except that each time it happens results in a project that doesn't live up to your expectations. Over time, disappointment accumulates until it feels like a routine part of knitting. Some people start to say, "Why bother?", and knit less and less. Others say that they are just not very good knitters, and believe it. They are wrong, of course: they are fine knitters, they just haven't been paying enough attention to gauge.

Most of the time when you make a gauge swatch, you are checking to see what needle size is right for you. Sometimes, though, you'll find out from the swatch that you are asking the yarn to do something it really doesn't want to. In that case, it is much better to find out immediately and choose a different yarn. If you have already bought enough for the project, you can usually go back to the shop and exchange all but the ball you have used (put that in your stash for a hat or part of your next multicolor project). Sometimes you can avoid this problem from the start by asking at the shop whether there is an open skein you can use to swatch.

Shops usually make a swatch for display purposes, and the remains of that skein may be in a basket somewhere. Chances are it will not be in your color, but you can experiment a bit. The display swatch can also tell you quite a bit. Assume the swatch represents the yarn's "home base," the middle of its range, the gauge the manufacturer recommends. You can choose to work it at a larger or smaller gauge, although the farther you wander from the "home base," the less predictable the results. Out at the edges of the possible (e.g. trying to knit a 4-stitches-to-the-inch yarn at 7, or at 3), success or failure is very individual. I know knitters who can knit very loosely while keeping the work even and regular; their fabrics look soft and drapey whereas others might just be sloppy. Other knitters always seem able to work yarns a little tighter while still getting pleasant, pliable fabrics. The lesson here? Until you know your own knitting style really well, do not take anyone else's word for it: swatch, *every* time.

The project for this chapter is a pair of socks. A lot of knitters—especially beginners—do not see the point of knitting socks. When you saw some really wonderful thing that made you say, "I've *got* to learn to knit," it was probably not a pair of socks. We just don't notice people's socks all that often. Even once the idea comes up—a pattern in a book, a class at a local shop—many knitters point out that socks cost about three dollars a pair at the mall and are therefore hardly worth making.

For older knitters, sock knitting may carry a lot of historical or emotional baggage. People who had to knit socks to keep the family's feet warm may remember it as drudgery, monotonous and purely utilitarian. During both World Wars, American knitters— including children and old men—produced socks by the thousands for servicemen. In the 1950s and '60s, it was fashionable for women to knit argyle socks for their husbands or boyfriends. (If you have never knit an argyle sock, you probably can't understand the kind of commitment this represented—and neither, by and large, did the boyfriends). For these knitters, making socks may always feel more like duty than pleasure.

Times have changed, though, and there are more good reasons to knit socks than ever. First, yarns have improved. It's true that you will probably pay more for the yarn than you would for the mass-produced socks, but it will be better yarn and they will be better socks. Yarn spun specifically for socks will be machine washable (some even machine dryable), with some nylon spun in for durability, and probably mostly wool (as opposed to cotton with acrylic in stores).

You want wool socks. They don't itch (you think your feet are so sensitive because they're ticklish, but they're being rubbed and chafed in shoes all day; they are not as sensitive as you think). And they're warm: unlike cotton, wool continues to insulate even when it is wet. (That's why people who spend time in boats want to wear them, even in summer.)

Socks that you make yourself will fit better than store-bought socks. You can make adjustments for that high arch, narrow heel, or thick calf. This kind of adaptation can, in turn, make your shoes fit better (especially work or hiking boots). If you have friends or family with special-needs feet, you can make gift socks that really show how well you know them: baby socks that won't fall off, ultra-warm alpaca socks, extra-extra-long socks. I know a knitter whose friend had a foot amputated because of diabetes. Knitting gorgeous, one-of-a-kind (literally) socks for that friend became a way of showing love and support.

And socks that you make yourself will look better than mass-produced socks. Sure, go ahead and make a couple of all-purpose pairs in denim blue or charcoal gray—but then look at the amazing space-dyed and spot-printed sock yarns out there today, and go wild. Make stripes with your leftovers. If you love purple and wear it often, you should have bright purple socks. Make cabled socks to wear with your Aran sweaters. Gave your father a hand-knit ski cap for his birthday last year? Chances are he needs matching socks this year.

Everything I've said so far about socks has focused on the product. But knitting socks is *fun*. It goes quickly, even if the pattern is complicated—there are just so many fewer stitches than in a sweater. Or even a sleeve. You can experiment with a new pattern or technique without the commitment of making a sweater. There's not enough time to get bored. Get used to the pattern, and presto! You're on to the next stage. (If you are really easily bored, make the second sock subtly different from the first.) And there's something intellectually satisfying about shaping fabric as you make it, creating perfect fit without waste or assembly.

The sock instructions given here are for standard, lightweight, fit-under-loafers socks. This is a versatile and useful weight. But lots of sock patterns use heavier yarn and larger needles to make boot socks or slipper socks. For socks to wear with shoes or boots, choose durable yarns. If you find something gorgeous, warm, and soft that you know will not withstand much abrasion (say, cashmere), make bed-socks or padding-around-the-house-in-the-evening socks.

And when you're choosing yarn for a specific pattern, don't be surprised if the yarn, gauge, and needles specified do not seem to match up: socks are often knit more densely than sweaters for greater durability. So if the pattern calls for a worsted-weight yarn that you are used to using with size 7 needles at 5 stitches to the inch, but the pattern recommends using size 4 needles and requires a gauge of 6 stitches to the inch, don't worry. The socks will be warmer and last longer than if you did the typical thing and used a sport-weight yarn at the same gauge. On the other hand, if you do not like knitting dense fabrics or if you find the perfect color in a sport-weight yarn, go ahead and use it. If the gauge is right, the socks will be fine. And as Elizabeth Zimmerman said, "You are the boss of your knitting."

PROJECT:
Socks

*This short sock has a small
motif in seed stitch worked from
the cuff down to the ankle.*

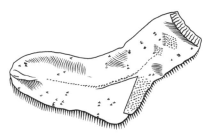

Size: Women's Medium

Materials: 250 yds sock or fingering-
weight yarn

       Size 1 dpn, or size to

          obtain gauge

Gauge: 8 sts = 1" in stockinette
stitch (i.e. knit every round). Note:
Most sock yarns recommend a gauge
of 7½ sts to the inch. These are
deliberately worked at a slightly
denser gauge for more durability
and pattern clarity.

Abbreviations: wyib: with yarn in
back. wyif: with yarn in front.

Cuff:

Holding 2 ndls together, cast on 64
sts. Remove 1 ndl. Divide sts onto 3
ndls and join, being careful not to
twist. Work in k1, p1 rib for 6 rnds.
Change to stockinette and work 6
more rnds. Next rnd: K16, p1, k31,
p1, k15. This sets position of chart
pattern: each p st is 7th st on Row 1

of chart. Work Chart Rnds 2–35,
repeating chart motif once at each
side of cuff, then rep rnds 34 and
35 until cuff measures 4½", ending
with Rnd 35.

Divide for heel:

K16, turn; p back across these 16
plus 15 more—31 sts on ndl. Heel
will be worked on these sts; ignore
all others for now.

Heel flap:

Row 1: *Slip 1 st purlwise wyib,
k1; rep from * to end of row, ending slip 1. **Row 2:** P. **Row 3:** *K1,
slip 1; rep from * to end of row,
ending k1. **Row 4:** P. Rep rows 1–4
until flap measures 2½", ending
with row 1 or 3.

Turn heel:

Next row: P18, p2tog, p1; turn, leaving rem 10 sts unworked.

Row 2: Slip 1 st purlwise wyib, k6, k2tog, k1; turn, leaving rem 10 sts unworked. **Row 3:** Slip 1 purlwise wyif, p7, p2tog, p1, turn (leaving 8 sts unworked). **Row 4:** Slip 1 wyib, k8, k2tog, k1, turn (8 sts rem).

Row 5: Slip 1 wyif, p9, p2tog, p1, turn (6 sts rem). **Row 6:** Slip 1 wyib, k10, k2tog, k1, turn (6 sts rem).

Row 7: Slip 1 wyif, p11, p2tog, p1, turn (4 sts rem). **Row 8:** Slip 1 wyib, k12, k2tog, k1, turn (4 sts rem).

Row 9: Slip 1 wyif, p13, p2tog, p1, turn (2 sts rem). **Row 10:** Slip 1 wyib, k14, k2tog, k1, turn (2 sts rem).

Row 11: Slip 1 wyif, p15, p2tog, p1, turn (no sts rem). **Row 12:** Slip 1 wyib, k16, k2tog, k1. 19 heel sts rem.

Rnd 35

Rnd 1

☐ knit
■ purl

Gusset:

Continue from the end of the last row down the left side of the heel flap. With an empty ndl, pick up and knit about 20 sts along heel flap. With another ndl, k across the 33 ignored sts (these will be called the instep sts). With another ndl, pick up and knit another 20 sts along right side of heel flap (these and the other picked-up sts will be called gusset sts). You have 92 sts on 4 ndls, and the round begins at the center of the heel. Now shape the gussets by decreasing as follows: K across heel sts; k to last 2 sts of gusset ndl, k2tog; across instep ndl, work p1, k31, p1; on second gusset ndl, ssk, k to end. K next rnd plain. Continue to work the decrease rnd every other rnd until 78 sts rem (that's 13 on each gusset ndl). Then work the decrease rnd every rnd until 64 sts rem (remembering to p the first and last instep sts on alt rnds to keep the "dot" pattern in place). At this point there are only 6 sts on each gusset ndl; it may be more comfortable to get rid of 1 ndl by dividing the heel sts onto the gusset ndls—10 sts to the left gusset ndl, 9 sts to the right.

Foot:
Work without further shaping until foot measures 6" from back of heel. Discontinue dot pattern; work in plain stockinette for another 1½", or approx. 1½" less than total length desired.

Shape toe:
Decrease as follows: At end of first ndl, k2tog; across instep ndl, k1, ssk, k to last 3 sts, k2tog, k1; at beg of last ndl, ssk, k to end. K 1 rnd plain. Work decrease rnd alternately with plain rnd 5 more times—40 sts

rem. Now decr every rnd 6 times—16 sts rem. Rearrange sts: Slip 1 st from either end of instep ndl to adjacent gusset ndl, then combine 2 gusset ndls onto 1; 8 sts on each of 2 ndls. Graft together using Kitchener st.

Chapter 9

Knitting on Your Own

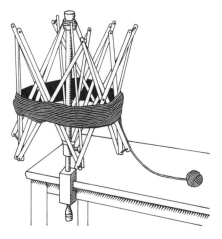

aybe you live alone. Maybe you only knit in your studio, or
on the train. Maybe you can't find a knitting group. If there
are other people in the room while you knit, but they don't knit,
you may feel more alone than when you're the only person in the
room. Whatever the reason, you may find yourself knitting alone
much of the time.

This isn't a bad thing.

Once you get the hang of it, knitting is a lovely rhythmic motion.
It can soothe and calm you. It can even put you into a meditative
trance. While your hands are busy, your mind can be emptied of
anxieties and details. Sometimes it may remain open and passive, in
a Zen-like state. Other times, it may float free in contemplation of

larger issues. Some knitters pick up a piece of simple work when they have a personal problem to sort out or a decision to make. Some knit while waiting for inspiration, whether for gift ideas or poems.

During my senior year in college, when I was working on my honors thesis, I stopped fighting my desire to knit (and my subsequent guilt about it). Instead, I would sit down with my knitting for fifteen or twenty minutes and start thinking about what I was writing and what I was going to write. Then I'd move to my desk, calm and focused and ready to go (fingers limber for the keyboard, too!), and write.

If I hit the kind of snag that used to leave my staring at the screen in frustration, periodically tapping the space bar to forestall the screensaver, I'd go back to the knitting.

When rereading the previous paragraph had completely undermined my confidence in my ability to say anything at all, I'd start knitting.

At those moments, which so often had ended in my closing the file and walking away stymied and disheartened, I'd go back to the knitting. Free of the distraction of what I had already written, soothed by familiar and repetitive motion, cheered by tangible proof of my ability to create something worthwhile, I would often be able to think past the difficulty and go back to writing. The sweater I was knitting at that time was black with a dark blue-green mohair, a gift for my friend Melissa, but I've always thought of it as the "thesis sweater," both because I knit it while writing my thesis and because it proved the thesis that knitting and schoolwork weren't mutually exclusive.

But notwithstanding an encouraging roommate and the evidence of a thriving yarn shop not five blocks away from my dorm room, I felt that I was knitting alone.

Well, not alone, exactly.

Often when I knit, I feel everyone else's fingers behind and before me—all those centuries, all those millions of knitters making things for their families or themselves, for necessity or for profit or for pleasure or all three. If I'm using a pattern, I feel the presence of the designer, and I sometimes have a sense that she and I are in dialogue for all the choices about technical details: "Why did she do it this way? What does she mean by that?" Some of my questions will be answered later in the pattern—"Aha! It didn't say to bind off when the back was finished because we're going to knit the shoulders together." Some things I only understand years later. For instance, the two different ways to decrease look different, and we use them when the decreases are going to show, so the raglan shaping is symmetrical. But unlike, say, grammar, the rules of which always seemed to me completely abstract and impersonal, the logic of knitting feels (to me, at least) intensely human.

So even at those points in my life when I did not have anyone to ask for help "live and in person," I still had a sense of context. Even my mistakes and misunderstandings are part of a tradition. (So are yours.) From this tradition comes, eventually, for many of us, the desire to branch out.

Here's how it usually happens: you're looking for a pattern for your next sweater, and you see something that's just right, except that you want a turtleneck and this one's a crewneck. You keep looking. And looking. But the other one is really perfect, except that it's not a turtleneck. So you turn to the yarn shop staff and say, "Is there any way I could turn this into a turtleneck?" And the shop-keeper says, "Sure." And now you're designing your own knitwear.

Here's a tip about necklines, by the way: the garment pieces are shaped the same whether the final neck is going to be a crewneck, rollneck, mock turtle, or turtle. The only difference is in what kind of edging you knit, and how much. Pick up stitches as instructed in the pattern, and then knit whatever you want—an inch of ribbing for a crewneck, 1 to 1½ inches of stockinette for a roll, maybe 2½ or 3 inches of a ribbing for a mock turtle, and 5 or 6 or more inches for the full turtleneck. (Elizabeth Zimmerman, in *Knitting Workshop,* gives these instructions for a turtleneck: "Knit up all stitches on a 16-inch needle and rib until you're sick and tired of it.") Now you are free to interchange round necks on any sweater you like.

Everybody has wanted to modify a pattern at some time or other. The most common reasons in my experience are fit and yarn suitability. "Fit" can mean simple issues of size, as when the pattern stops at twenty-four months but you want to knit it for the fall for a baby who'll be two in July. But it also covers aesthetic matters: the wearer is narrow at the shoulders but wide at the hips, so either the top or the bottom looks bad on standard sizes, or a band of patterning at the bottom is guaranteed to be unflattering. Adjustments to the yarn are usually for fiber ("It's shown in wool; can I substitute cotton?") or gauge ("I like the blue in this worsted-weight, but the pattern calls for sport"). Then there are the easy omissions: can I make this sweater but skip the complicated fair-isle border? Do I have to use the contrast-color faux-fur trim? What is that nonsense with the ruffle around the neck?

The short answer to questions like these is "yes." Yes, you can change anything you dislike about a sweater. Some of the changes may require some assistance from someone with a little more experience. Some, such as big changes in gauge, may be so complex that it's simpler to start with a different pattern. But yes, you can change whatever you want.

The transition from modifying existing patterns to designing your own isn't the big leap you might imagine. After you've been making changes to published patterns for awhile, you may get an idea and not be able to find a pattern that looks much like it.

Or you'll try to work with the nearest thing, and start to think, "You know, it would be simpler to start from scratch." And indeed, starting from scratch isn't a bad idea.

When Nadia Severns, a professional knitwear designer for several major yarn companies whose work routinely appears in national knitting magazines, begins work on a project, she asks herself, "What am I trying to say with this design?" She may focus on the time or place where the garment is likely to be worn, or on outside source material. She is often inspired by antique textiles, especially carpets (Oriental or Native American). She may make some sketches, but more often she moves directly to charts—graphs that indicate color placement for multicolor designs, or size and spacing of cables or other textural elements. "And then I swatch," she says, "and swatch." It can take weeks or months to get the pattern just right. Meanwhile, yarn and books "are piled all over the house—the kids know not to touch."

Publication schedules don't always allow for this kind of process, however. Yarn companies may send specific yarns and request a complete garment—with instructions for three sizes—within three weeks. At times like this, a design idea that isn't working right away may be put aside for later reconsideration.

My recommended process for learning to design is pretty down-to-earth and hands-on; I'm a pragmatist. For a wonderful book with a very different approach, see Deborah Newton's *Designing Knitwear*. But if you don't know how to draw or how to sew, if you're interested in making a particular sweater rather than training your eye or developing a portfolio, this is how I go about it.

First, steal whenever possible. That is, start with a professional pattern if you can. Later, when you have more experience, you'll know how wide a neckline should be, how deep an armhole, how wide a rib. For now, trust designers who've been doing this for awhile.

Second, compare sources. By looking at several versions of the same thing, you can often figure out where a particular number comes from. For instance, if you're modifying a cardigan pattern, you may wonder whether buttonholes should always be 3 inches apart, or whether that's just what happens when you space seven buttons evenly up the front of a 21-inch-long sweater. Look at the other sizes in this pattern first—probably there are slightly shorter or longer sizes that tell you to make buttonholes at slightly different intervals. Then find another cardigan pattern—are there still seven buttons?

Where possible, compare similar types of pattern—if your cardigan is a little close-fitting job, like the outer piece in a traditional twinset, the number of buttons on a three-quarter-length jacket may not be very significant.

Third, practice guessing where certain numbers come from, and learn the most common explanations. This is really the puzzling part. I'm going to do what I can to demystify it.

Almost every sweater begins with a chest measurement. How big around do you want the garment to be at the underarm, before any armhole shaping begins? Use this measurement in inches or centimeters, whichever is more comfortable for you. Divide the number in half to get the width of the back. Multiply the result by your gauge—the number of stitches per inch (or centimeter) your yarn gets for you on the needles you want to use in the pattern stitch you have in mind. (You did do a gauge swatch, didn't you? If you have any doubts about this, review Chapter 8 and then come back.) This number is pretty much the number of stitches you want for the back—except that it's probably something like 87.39, which is difficult to cast on. Obviously, you have to round that number off.

Now think like a knitter: it's closer to 87 than 88, yes, but if you're going to work a rib at the bottom, an even number will be much better. And if the body is done in a pattern that's a multiple of five, you'd really rather have 90. But if you want the rib to fit snugly, choose a smaller number—probably 82 or 84—and then plan to increase to 90 when you start the pattern.

When a set of instructions tells you to cast on or bind off or increase or decrease a number of stitches, that number has almost always come from a measurement. The instructions to "bind off 4 sts at beg of next 2 rows" for armhole shaping have nothing to do with the sacred number 4 and everything to do with the fact that the sweater is knit at a gauge of 4 stitches to the inch. Typical armhole shapings begin by binding off 1 inch worth of stitches. How do you know this? Because I said so. How do I know? Because I compared a lot of patterns with armhole shaping and noticed that they almost all did the same thing, whether they were children's or adults' sweaters.

So if you are modifying a pattern that is written for bulky-weight yarn at 3 stitches to an inch so you can knit it out of a different yarn at 4 stitches to an inch, you are basically going to convert a lot of numbers to inches and then back to stitch numbers. The lengths won't change—they're already in inches. But when the neck shaping says to "bind off center 18 sts, then dec 1 st at each neck edge every other row 3 times," you're going to reason as follows: 18 stitches at their gauge is 6 inches; 6 inches at my gauge is 24 stitches; I need to bind off the center 24 stitches. Then they decrease 1 stitch at each edge 3 times—that's 3 stitches at each side, or 1 inch, which for me is 4 stitches. So I decrease 1 stitch at each side of the neck 4 times, for a total neck width of 32 stitches, or 8 inches.

You may worry that since you have to work 4 decreases where the pattern only worked 3, you are going to need 8 rows where they used 6—is this a problem? Short answer: probably not, since 2 rows isn't a big difference and your rows are probably a little smaller than theirs anyway.

Still worried? Double-check this way: go back to your gauge swatch and see how long 8 rows is—probably about 1½ inches. Now look at where those neck shaping instructions begin: "Work even until piece meas 2 inches less than back to shoulder. Shape neck." So as long as your revised neck shaping doesn't take longer than 2 inches, you're still on schedule. (What to do if the numbers were different and your neck shaping was likely to take 2½ inches? Start the neck shaping when front measures 2½ inches less than back to shoulder, that's all.)

It really is that simple. I would, however, like to say a word about a slightly tricky bit: sleeves. (This is important stuff even if you don't modify patterns or design your own yet, because often sleeves do not come out right even if you follow the instructions religiously.) Think of a sleeve as almost a triangle: there's the narrow part at the bottom, the wide part at the top, and the long part in between. Most patterns tell you to increase a certain number of times, and they tell you how often to do it, and they tell you how long the sleeve should be altogether: "Incr 1 st each end every 4 rows 23 times (92 sts); work even until piece meas 18" or desired length." And every few days somebody calls me to say either "My sleeve is the right length but I haven't finished increasing yet" or "My sleeve is too long, but all I did was increase the way it said to." The problem here is *vertical gauge*—how many rows to the inch the designer got versus how many the knitter did. If you are already at the specified length but you have not done the specified number of increases, you are getting fewer rows per inch than the pattern assumes.

What to do? Even if you'd noticed this when you measured your initial swatch, there wouldn't have been anything to do about it—changing needle size would have affected your horizontal gauge (stitches per inch), which was correct. No, you need to recalculate your increase rate.

Here's how: start with the sleeve length from that "until sleeve measures 18 inches" part. Subtract the measurement of any cuff ribbing or edging. Subtract another inch as a margin of error. The remainder is the length you have in which to accomplish the number of increases you need. Convert that length to rows by multiplying by your row gauge. Now you know that you need to increase, say, 23 times in 60 rows. Divide 60 by 23—increase every 2.61 rows? Not likely. Increase every 2 rows? That would take 46 rows, leaving a lot left over. Every 3 rows? Takes 69 rows, 9 rows too many; that's the problem you had last time. Solution? Do some of each—increase every other row maybe 10 times (20 rows) then every third row the other 13 times (39 rows)—a total of 59 rows, right on target.

Here's a funny thing about modern knitting patterns, though: they'll almost never tell you to work shaping at intervals of odd numbers of rows—it's every second row, or every fourth or sixth, but you're not going to see instructions to increase every third row. I don't know why this is. My suspicion is that they think we'd rather increase on right-side rows only, and that we'd get hopelessly confused if the increases came up sometimes on right-side rows and sometimes on wrong-side rows (as they will if the intervals aren't all even numbers). If you aren't scared of increasing on wrong-side rows—and I don't know any reason why you should be—go right ahead. If you are, work some increases every second row and the rest every fourth.

That's how to calculate (or recalculate) sleeve increases. I've seen so many cases where people ran into trouble following the instructions as given that I really recommend that you check your vertical gauge against the directions before you start knitting the sleeves on any sweater. It doesn't take long, the math isn't all that tough if you have to make an adjustment, and it is extremely frustrating to discover the problem later. (By the way, the options if you *do* find the problem later are: One, decide to fudge in either direction—slightly longer or narrower sleeve is okay. Two, rip back partway and start increasing faster—how far and how fast depends on how far off the original instructions are.)

The design at the end of this chapter is for a beret and mitten set. Here's a little history behind its development.

I started with the yarn: Grignasco's "Top Print," pure alpaca. It has an unusual color effect; the yarn has three plies, each of which is variegated, so any given inch will have two or three colors twisted together. Because it is alpaca, it is very warm and soft. Because it's from Grignasco, it is fairly expensive. We'd had it at the shop last winter in four color combinations and people loved it, so this season we ordered ten colors.

But there was still some question about what to make with it. Last year there were a lot of scarves but not much else. It is too warm and too expensive for most sweaters (though I've since seen some beautiful designs using it that way), too fragile for socks. As I thought about accessories and other small projects, a hat and mittens both seemed like good possibilities (as opposed to a bag, which would stretch out of shape, or a pillow, which would waste the lovely feel and warmth).

We have quite a few hat patterns at the shop. The most common request is for a plain skullcap (see the Watch Cap at the end of Chapter 7, page 87), but the next most frequent is the call for a woman's hat that won't muss the wearer's hair. I decided to try for a large soft beret shape, something more like a brioche than a tam. The stitch pattern had to be very simple, both for the proper drape of the fabric and because the color effect makes the yarn pretty busy in itself. Stockinette seemed fine, but a little boring. As I thought about the band, I considered other beret patterns I'd seen.

Many had garter-stitch bands, which I never like, because the cast-on edge is usually too tight but the rest of the band doesn't hold very well. I didn't think a usual ribbing would be much better, though, because it seemed likely to be too loose (alpaca can be sort of limp; it has a tendency to stretch and stay stretched).

This is a stage where I might have swatched some possible band treatments to look them over. As it happened, I had a hunch about another possibility that solved several problems at once: a cabled band. Some knitting textbooks point out that cable patterns are technically ribbed fabrics since the knit ropes alternate with a purl background. While I acknowledge that this is true for simple, repeating cables (though not, for instance, for lattices), it had never seemed very interesting. Now, however, I had a use for the fact. Instead of alternating plain knit stitches with purls in my band, I would alternate small cables with a pair of purls. The fabric would have some "give" but be tighter than plain (or even twisted) ribbing would be, I reasoned, thus helping the alpaca keep its shape. I would make the band deeper than the usual inch so that more cabling would show.

At this point, I began to swatch, because now I needed information rather than theory. Would the cable pattern behave as I thought? And what kind of gauge would it give? (Top Print is usually nice at about 5 or 5½ stitches to the inch for a scarf, but this would clearly be very different.) Depending on how much stretch the cables actually had, should I plan to write instructions for more than one size, or would one set of numbers stretch to accommodate a variety of adult heads? And what about after the band—how big would the crown be when I shifted to stockinette? Most beret instructions require increasing after the band (whether gradually or all at once), but I might actually have to decrease in this case.

My swatch used size 3 needles and was about 30 stitches wide—5 cables, which turned out to be about 3 inches. That would be way too small a swatch if I were planning a sweater, but I felt it gave me enough to go on for the hat. (What's the difference, you ask? If I made a miscalculation because my swatch was too small to be accurate, I'd be less annoyed about having to rip and rework the hat than I would be for something the size of a sweater.) After working the cable pattern until the ropes had twisted 3 times, I changed to size 6 needles and stockinette. The swatch immediately got much larger; I had to knit for several more inches before I could get an accurate measurement.

I liked the look and feel of both sections of the swatch. When I started to measure, I found that the stockinette area was about 5 stitches to the inch, while the cable area was more like 9. (See what I mean about how much cables pull the fabric in?) I also measured the cable area stretched as wide as seemed comfortable, bearing in mind that a too-tight hatband is unpleasant and crushes the hair, and this time I got 7 stitches to the inch. I also observed that the cast-on row was much tighter than the rest of the swatch.

Time for some calculations. Most women's hat patterns have 21-inch circumferences; one of my customers asserts that her head is very large, and it measures 22 inches. The number of stitches had to be a multiple of six for the cable pattern to work out. I needed numbers that were less than 21 times 9 (the band so relaxed that it would fall into an average wearer's eyes) and more than 22 times 7 (the band at maximum stretch to fit the large head). This gave me a range from 154 to 189.

Now I considered the size of the crown, the stockinette part of the hat. At a gauge of 5 stitches to the inch, 189 stitches would give the beret a maximum circumference of nearly 38 inches, or (quick flashback to geometry class to figure out the diameter of a circle from the circumference—divide by pi) more than 12 inches across. In other words, my "brioche" was going to be the size of a medium pizza.

Back to the drawing board.

What about numbers at the lower end of the range? Well, 154 stitches would be a 30-inch circumference, just under 10 inches across the top. This seemed acceptable. The nearest multiple of six is 156. I worried that this was too close to the minimum necessary for Bev's head, but I took the chance. (You may ask: wouldn't it have been better to use more stitches in the band to be safe, and then decrease after the band to keep the crown from being too large? Well, yes and no. The fit might have been more precise, but I wanted to keep the knitting simple, and I really liked the idea of making the shift in stitch pattern do all the shaping work.)

The rest of the calculations went more quickly. I looked at a few other beret patterns and chose a depth before the decreasing for the top began, using something from the larger end of the range to match my large-ish crown. The top decreases were easier than one might expect, because I know a few general rules of hat shaping. For instance, if you do not want to have to think much about it, most hats come out fine if you decrease 5 or 6 times evenly spaced around. And if you want a not-quite-flat beret top, you do the first half of the decreases every other round and the second half every round. (For those of you who aren't afraid of a little math: first, figure out how many decrease rounds you will need. If you start with 156 stitches and decrease 6 each time, you'll decrease 26 times—divide 156 by 6—to wind up with 6 stitches at the center. Then, figure out how many rounds you'll need to fill the space from the outer edge of the hat to the center—multiply the radius of the circle by your row gauge—in this case 5" times 6. For a perfectly flat top, use this number of rounds to accomplish your decreases, that is, 26 decreases spread evenly over 30 rounds. For a more domed top, arrange to work more rounds, in this case 35. The reason this so often works out to 5 or 6 decreases per round, worked alternately for the first half and consecutively for the second, has to do with the ratio of stitches to rows per inch for the typical stockinette gauge.)

After this, the mittens were easy: a slightly tighter gauge for greater warmth and durability, necessary decreases from cuff to hand (don't want any balloon here!), typical thumb gusset. The finished product came out a little small, but adding stitches would have thrown off the very tidy numbers, so instead I recommended knitting a little looser for larger sizes.

One last thing about the design process for this set: with ten colors to choose from, how did I end up selecting a berry-red yarn? The important thing was knowing that the finished product would be on display in the shop. Conventional retail wisdom has it that one should display a bright, attention-grabbing color—easy enough for the customer to decide she'd rather have the pearl gray than the screaming green once she's noticed the item in the first place. So that ruled out the darker and subtler colors.

Then at the shop we try to sample colors that aren't going to be tremendously popular, both because a model can call attention to an otherwise overlooked color, and because it is better to sell the popular colors to people who want them rather than using them in display pieces (which are not for sale). The red is less glamorous than most of the Top Print colors; it is variegated in shades of red, where a typical colorway would include, say, brown, green, and gold. In addition, fashion forecasting said that red was going to be "hot."

That did it: red it was.

PROJECT:
Beret and Mitten set

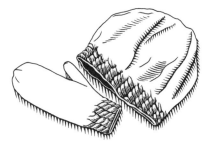

Size:

Hat: Women's Medium, but should fit most

Mittens: Women's Small. For Women's Medium, work body of mittens on Size 6 dpn instead of Size 5.

Materials: 3 sk Grignasco "Top Print" (about 1½ for hat, 1½ for mittens), or 350 yds of any light-worsted weight alpaca

    cable ndl

    2 ring markers

    small stitch holder

    16" circular ndl size 3, or size
        to obtain gauge

    16" circular ndl size 6, or size
        to obtain gauge

    Size 3, 5, and 6 dpn, or sizes
        to obtain gauge

Gauges: 9 sts = 1" over cable pattern on smallest ndls, relaxed

    7 sts = 1" over cable pattern
        on smallest ndls, stretched

    5 sts and 6 rows = 1" over
        stockinette st on largest ndls

Cable Pattern (multiple of 6 sts):

Round 1: *P1, slip next 2 sts to cable ndl and hold at front of work, k2, k2 from cable ndl, p1; rep from * to end of rnd. **Rnds 2, 3, and 4:** *P1, k4, p1; rep from * to end of rnd. Rep Rnds 1–4 for Cable Pattern.

Beret:

Using larger circular ndl, cast on 156 sts. Change to smaller circular ndl and work 18 rnds of Cable Pattern, thus ending with Rnd 2. Change to larger circular ndl and stockinette st (i.e. knit every rnd). When piece meas 5" from cast-on, begin decr for top, changing to largest dpn when necessary:

    Rnd 1: (K24, k2tog) 6 times (150 sts rem). **Rnds 2, 4, 6, 8, 10,**

12, 14, 16, 18, and 20: Knit.

Rnd 3: (K23, k2tog) around.

Rnd 5: (K22, k2tog) around.

Rnd 7: (K21, k2tog) around.

Rnd 9: (K20, k2tog) around.

Rnd 11: (K19, k2tog) around.

Rnd 13: (K18, k2tog) around.

Rnd 15: (K17, k2tog) around.

Rnd 17: (K16, k2tog) around.

Rnd 19: (K15, k2tog) around.

Rnd 21: (K14, k2tog) around (90 sts rem).

From this point on, decr every rnd. **Rnd 22:** (K13, k2tog) around.

Rnd 23: (K12, k2tog) around.

Rnd 24: (K11, k2tog) around.

Rnd 25: (K10, k2tog) around.

Rnd 26: (K9, k2tog) around.

Rnd 27: (K8, k2tog) around.

Rnd 28: (K7, k2tog) around.

Rnd 29: (K6, k2tog) around.

Rnd 30: (K5, k2tog) around.

Rnd 31: (K4, k2tog) around.

Rnd 32: (K3, k2tog) around.

Rnd 33: (K2, k2tog) around.

Rnd 34: (K1, k2tog) around.

Rnd 35: K2tog 6 times. Cut yarn, leaving about 6" tail. Thread through rem 6 sts and fasten off. Work in ends.

Left Mitten:

Using smallest dpn, cast on 54 sts. Work Cable Pattern for 18 rnds. Change to middle-size dpn and decr as follows: (K1, k2tog) around (36 sts). Knit 3 rnds.** Establish thumb gusset: K16, pm, m1, k1, m1, pm, k19. *Knit 2 rnds without shaping. Incr rnd: K to first marker, slip marker, m1, k to second marker, m1, slip marker, k to end of rnd. Rep from * 3 more times—there should be 11 sts between markers. Knit 2 rnds. Next rnd: Knit to marker, remove marker, slip next 11 sts to holder, cast on 5 sts, remove second marker, k to end of rnd (40 sts). Next rnd: K15, ssk, k3, k2tog, k to end of rnd. Next rnd: K15, ssk, k1, k2tog, k to end of rnd (36 sts). Work even on these sts until mitten reaches tip of second-longest finger (about 8¼" from cast-on for Women's Small).

Shape top:

Rnd 1: (K4, k2tog) 6 times (30 sts rem). **Rnds 2 and 4:** Knit. **Rnd 3:** (K3, k2tog) around. **Rnd 5:** (K2, k2tog) around. **Rnd 6:** (K1, k2tog)

around. **Rnd 7:** K2tog 6 times. Cut
yarn, leaving about 6" tail. Thread
through rem 6 sts and fasten off.

Thumb:
Replace 11 sts from holder onto 2
ndls. Using another dpn (from now
on called "Ndl 3"), pick up and k 7
sts along upper edge of thumb hole.
Knit across ndls 1 and 2. Ndl 3:
Ssk, k3, k2tog. Knit across ndls 1
and 2 again. Ndl 3: Ssk, k1, k2tog.
Work even on these 14 sts until
thumb is about 2 rnds longer than
tip of thumb—about 2" from
picked-up sts for Women's Small.
Shape top: K2tog around. Cut yarn,
leaving about 6" tail. Thread
through rem 7 sts and fasten off.
Work in ends.

Right Mitten:
Work as for Left Mitten until **.
Establish thumb gusset: K19, pm,
m1, k1, m1, pm, k to end of rnd.
Shape gusset as for left mitten.
(When decr cast-on sts after putting
gusset sts on holder, k18, then work
decs.) Finish as for left mitten.

Chapter 10

Knitting in
the Computer Age

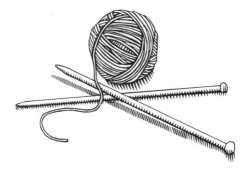

First of all, stop thinking the two have nothing to do with each other! The connections may not seem obvious at first, but there is quite a bit to say. Lots of people do both. For some, it's the contrast that satisfies: after a long day of abstract cerebral work, all one wants is the tactile experience of knitting, with its immediate, tangible results. On the other hand, here's something that knitting and computers have in common: their legions of fans aren't always who you expect. Your grandmother sends you e-mail. The young woman on the bus with the pierced eyebrow is knitting mittens. And lastly, insofar as computers seem to touch every aspect of human life now, there's *got* to be computer stuff for knitters. Good stuff.

And, indeed, there is. A CD-Rom is available to teach knitting basics, with plenty of visuals to show hand positions for tricky maneuvers like the long-tail cast-on. Several software packages for home computers speed up and simplify the process of designing sweaters. Professionals can use them to eliminate a lot of the tedious math that takes a sketch to a set of instructions. Individual knitters can use them to customize fit or produce simple patterns for whatever yarn is on hand.

Any simple paintbox program can be a valuable resource for a knitter who likes color patterns. You can create an image, or scan one from some other source, and then manipulate it to your heart's content—change scale or color, rotate it to a different angle, make multiple copies. There are knitting- or needlework-specific programs, which will turn the results into a chart or graph. Some of the applications for this kind of thing are obvious—you can take an existing knitting design and see what happens if you change one or more colors; you can isolate one motif from a complicated sweater and enlarge or repeat it for use alone. You could also, however, adapt your favorite Matisse painting or your kid's latest drawing.

There's software available to help you inventory your stash. This may seem like a pointless exercise. Why boot up the computer instead of just going down to the basement to see how many skeins of the stuff you have? And who wants to go to the trouble of updating a spreadsheet after every purchase or project? The payoff comes if you have a Personal Digital Assistant like the Palm Pilot. Now your inventory is literally on hand when you're in a shop and see a great new pattern—do you have enough Newport for this cardigan? The PDA not only knows how many skeins you have, it knows how many yards per skein in Sand, which is the yarn the pattern calls for. Or if you're buying a new project and cannot remember whether you already have a 24-inch-long size 2 needle, your PDA can tell you.

And as with any organizer, you can make your own files to store information that's useful to you. What was your dad's chest measurement again? And, conversely, you can make a list of key sweater-fit measurements—chest circumference, length to shoulder, arm length—and update your nieces' numbers the next time you see them.

Take it one step further: make yourself a knitting journal. This has always been a good idea for a notebook—you can create a new page for every project, with information about size, pattern, yarn requirements, needle size, any changes you made to the pattern, recipient and date or occasion, and notes about fit or changes you'd want to make next time. You can even attach a swatch (if possible) or at least a piece of the yarn. You can do everything except the swatch on your computer, and then you can keep it with you for easy reference.

Can't remember whether you made your brother blue socks or gray last year? Check.

Can't remember whether you used a size 7 needle or a size 8 with this yarn, or what gauge it gave you? Check.

Fancy a pattern, but think the designer is the same as the one whose instructions drove you nuts last time? Check.

Meet someone who is making the same sweater you made a couple years back, and think you remember needing one more skein of yarn than the pattern called for? Check, and tell her so.

It doesn't take long to make notes of this kind for a project, and you will love having the information available all the time.

I love my Filofax, but frankly, these new applications are making me think seriously about switching to the PDA.

For the vast majority of knitters with computers, of course, the major intersection between the two is the Internet. The World Wide Web is the new century's means of exchange for goods and information—both of which are key for knitters. Retail opportunities abound on the Internet: there are bricks-and-mortar yarn shops with retail websites, catalog companies who are now displaying their wares online, and new Web-based mail-order sources. Whatever you can't get at your local yarn shop can be found on the Internet. If a magazine uses a yarn you've never heard of for a sweater you like, and your local shop does not carry it, you can go online and find someone who will send it to you. If you're just thinking it over, you may find that the manufacturer or distributor of the yarn has a site complete with color cards. There is no need to restrict yourself to the color shown in the picture, or to rely on descriptives like "light blue" or "sand." If it is time to complete your set of rosewood double-pointed needles, but your shop reports that size 13 is backordered, you can probably find a source on the Web that has them in stock.

But before you put down this book and run for your credit card, let me add a few words of caution. First, buying knitting supplies online has the same problems as all other online retail ventures. You must rely on the security of the site to protect you against credit-card fraud. Shipping charges may increase the cost of your purchase considerably. Returns and exchanges are inconvenient and can be costly.

Plus there are a few difficulties specific to knitting. We seldom choose yarn by appearance alone; pictures on a website cannot tell you how a yarn feels in the hand. Color doesn't reproduce accurately on a computer. No matter how carefully the site designer has adjusted the display, it will appear different on just about every monitor. And online customer service can never provide the kind of help that a physical shop does: even if you can e-mail the vendor for an explanation of an unfamiliar pattern term, you can't show her the work and say, "What am I doing wrong?"

From time to time, you may know exactly what you want to buy online—a kit from a familiar source, another color of a yarn you have used many times, those backordered needles. These are fairly safe purchases. But I'd like to ask you to consider the consequences of your actions. If you want to be able to go to a shop for classes, or to get help with a new technique; if you want to be able to see new types of yarn in person, touch a swatch made from one, hold a skein up beside your face and ask, "Do you think this color works for me?"; if you want the convenience of running out on your lunch hour to replace a lost needle, rather than waiting three days for UPS—if you want to have a local yarn shop, you have to patronize it.

That said, there are knitting supplies available on the net that I wouldn't want anyone to pass up. When you need one more skein of something that you bought at your local shop's end-of-season sale last year, go online to look for it. (The shop usually has to get ten or more skeins at a time, and if they wanted to have the yarn around, they probably would not have been closing it out last year.) Sometimes a yarn or a color has been discontinued, or you need to match an old dye lot. Someone on the Internet likely has it.

There are an awful lot of knitting patterns available on the Web—and I don't just mean "through the Web," patterns you find, pay for, and receive in the mail (although there are an awful lot of those, too). But there are also many, many patterns free for the downloading. It seems that plenty of knitters want to share their ideas. So they put their designs up on a page and wait for people to happen by. Sometimes a number of pages will get linked to one another in a "pattern ring;" once you've found one, it will lead you to lots of others. As with everything on the Web, there is no central authority monitoring these patterns for accuracy; they may be missing information that's important (like how much yarn is required) or crucial (like gauge). Or there may be a mistake in the instructions. But if you are willing to work through the bugs, you can find all sorts of fun and funky things.

Commercial sites—retail stores, magazines, or yarn companies—may also offer free patterns as incentives for knitters to frequent a site. These are usually more professional, following standard pattern formats and careful proofreading habits.

The Web is a treasure trove of old pattern books and magazines: copies of *Vogue Knitting* from the 1950s are changing hands through eBay and other online auction sites, and there are "pattern museums" with nineteenth- and early twentieth-century sources. This use of the Web thrills me: irreplaceable old magazines that would once have crumbled to dust in attics or been put out with the trash now find their way into the collections of people who will care for them. Libraries and museums are starved for space and cannot be bothered with such "trivia."

We will have to be our own archivists in order to preserve our knitting heritage. You do not have to log on to eBay to do your part. Put the word out to friends and family that you will make or find a home for old knitting patterns. When people clean out basements or get ready to move a grandmother to an apartment, remind them to be on the lookout for such things. If you can't store these treasures, ask your local shop if it already maintains an archive or would consider finding room for one, and if not, whether it would let you post a notice that you've got vintage patterns available to anyone who will provide a good home. If all else fails, put them on eBay yourself as the seller and wait for someone with more space to bid for the privilege of being a custodian of knitting history.

Buying patterns through an online auction house means using the Internet as a way of exchanging information that is printed on paper. The great efficiency of the net, though, is that it *removes* paper. So take the next step: use the Internet to exchange knitting information.

Here's a fairly common type of knitting question: how many yards are there in a skein of the yarn called "Isis?" There are a number of ways you could use the net to answer the question. Go to the Web site run by Colinette, the yarn's manufacturer. If the site

KNITTING IN THE COMPUTER AGE

doesn't have the yardage, either because length per skein is not included in the information about the yarn or because the length is in meters and you don't know how to convert it to yards, go to the Web site run by Unique Kolours, the U.S. distributor of the yarn. If the information isn't posted clearly there, e-mail the Web site with the question, or use the links to retail shops that carry Colinette yarns. Or you could go to the Knit List homepage and search its online yarn reviews for "Isis." The review will also give you washing instructions, gauge, suggested needle size, and what one or more knitters had to say about the experience of using the yarn—did it split? pill? fade? slide through the fingers like liquid silk?

Or you could post the question to the usenet newsgroup rec.crafts.textiles.yarn, a sort of bulletin board discussion group for all things yarn-related. Someone reading the postings will have a skein on hand, and they'll check the label and post the answer. While you're waiting, you can read about sources for good patterns for knitting or crocheting a teddy bear or a tea cozy, and maybe, for instance, scroll through a discussion about what reactions people get when they knit in public in Chicago.

Or you could subscribe to the Knit List (www.kniton.com) or KnitU (www.knittinguniverse.com/knitu/index.taf) or one of a dozen other knitting listervers. These automated mailing lists send your e-mail to every subscriber; you receive a copy in your mailbox of everything sent to the list, either as each message comes in or in large batches (called "digests"). When you ask about the yardage of Isis on the Knit List, someone there too will be more than willing to check the yardage on a skein at home—but he or she will likely be pre-empted by someone who knows the yardage off the top of her head.

These are really high-traffic lists: you may receive eighty or more messages *a day* from either one. And their subscribers number in the thousands, so the accumulated knitting wisdom among the knitters is staggering. KnitU adds to this expertise by featuring "guest speakers," big-name experts who sit in on the list for a few weeks at a time and field questions both specific and general. There are special-interest listservers for sock knitting, Aran knitting, lace knitting, those who use knitting machines, and gay/lesbian/bisexual knitters, among others.

Lists also differ from one another in terms of how much "chat," or non-knitting material, they find acceptable. Some lists deliberately define themselves as highly technical; others like to feel more "friendly" by welcoming knitting spin-off topics—like the impact of a knitted baby gift on one's relationship with a sister-in-law, or commiseration about living with a husband who won't wear sweaters.

The various knitting mailing lists have become full-fledged online knitting communities, and they do almost everything your local knitting circle does: knitters help and inspire one another, compare notes on tools and techniques, and discuss the role of knitting in our lives and in the world at large. For several years, members of the Knit List have held a pattern exchange around the winter holidays, posting original patterns for gift projects to the list as their gifts to one another. (These patterns are archived at the Knit List Web site.) When members attend popular fiber events like Stitches or the Maryland Sheep and Wool Festival, they wear bright blue, hand-knitted, miniature socks pinned to their lapels so as to identify each other ("Oh! *You're* 'KnitCat@aol'!"). If you're going to Boston on business, any Internet search engine can help you find the knitting shops there, and the Knitters magazine site (www.knittinguniverse.com) will provide listings that include the shops' hours and some information about what they stock. The Knit List, however, will tell you which shop local knitters like best and if it's important to go in the afternoon and ask for Judy.

One of the best knitting Web sites is Woolworks.org, built and maintained by Emily Way. There's a comprehensive list of knitting listservers, a shop directory, free patterns, a gallery with photos of Emily's work and links to other people's, a list of charities seeking donations of knitted items, and much more—up to and including links to sheep-themed screensavers and wallpaper for your home computer.

As I watched a demo for a screensaver featuring cartoon sheep floating down out of the sky onto a meadow, it occurred to me that knitting and computers are a perfect match. The advanced technology brings an old craft into the twenty-first century. And fiberwork makes a hard-edged, digital universe much more "warm and fuzzy."

PROJECT:
Palm Pilot Cover

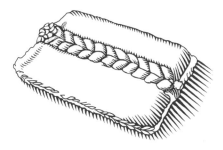

Why not make a case for your Palm Pilot or other PDA? They all seem to come with cases anyway—just not very nice ones. (And if you reduce the 6-st purl panels to 5 sts each, the size is right for a cell-phone cover.) This has a braided cable up the front and back, with a knit-in button and buttonhole at the top.

The yarn specified is perfect for the project: strong, shiny, durable, with lovely luminous colors. It's a big skein, though, so you'll have enough to make several "Palm sweaters."

Size: About 4" x 5¼", but flexible enough to accommodate most PDAs
Materials: 1 sk Classic Elite "Provence," or about 50 yds of any DK-weight cotton
    Size 5 ndls, or size to obtain gauge
    Cable ndl

Gauge: 5¼ sts = 1" over reverse stockinette

Palm Pilot Cover:
Cast on 42 sts. Work in pattern as follows:

Row 1 (and all WS rows): P2, *k6, p6, k6, p2; rep from * once.
Row 2: K2, *p6, slip 2 sts to cable ndl and hold at back of work, k2, k2 from cable ndl, k2, p6, k2; rep from *. **Row 4:** K2, *p6, k2, slip 2 sts to cable ndl and hold at front of work, k2, k2 from cable ndl, p6, k2; rep from *. Rep these 4 rows until piece meas 5½" from beg, ending with a RS row. Next row: P2, k6, p2, p2tog, p2, k6, p2; k6, p6, k6, p2.

Bobble and buttonhole row:
[Note: here's what to do when the instructions in this row say "make bobble": k1, yo, k1, yo, k1, *all* into the next st. Turn the work around and k5. Turn, p5. Turn, k5. Turn, sl 2, k2tog, pass 1 slipped st over, return the last st on the right ndl to the left ndl, pass 2nd st on left ndl over 1st and off the end of the ndl, return first st on left ndl to right ndl, pass slipped st over. You're back to the 1 st you started with.]
K2, p6, k1, k2tog, yo 3 times, k2tog, k1, p6, k2; p6, k2, make bobble, k2, p6, k2.

Next row: Bind off all sts purlwise, working (p1, k1, p1) into the triple yarnover from the previous row.

Finishing: Sew side and bottom seams. Weave in ends.

Chapter 11

Knitting in the Global Village

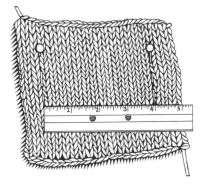

Once upon a time, knitters used local wools and knit in the
patterns traditional to their own village or region, using
techniques that stayed constant and consistent for generations.
From one region to another, however, huge variations developed.
Knitters from the British Isles carried the yarn in their right hand
(and still do), "Continental" knitters in their left. All over Western
Europe, socks are begun at the cuff and knit down toward the toe;
in the Balkan states and points south and east, one starts at the
toe and knits northward. Greek and Italian knitters—and those
from the Andes—tension their working yarn by running it up
and around the back of their necks.

Once, knitters might have seen a new pattern stitch on a traveler's hat and copied or adapted it into their own repertoire. Now,

travel is quick and easy. Books circulate around the world, and the Internet moves information in an instant. At the same time, the technological advances of the last century that turned knitting from a routine necessity into a hobby in the United States have also changed traditional ways of life elsewhere, and local knitting traditions are in danger of dying out. The race is on between the forces of "modernization" and those who would preserve the broadest possible diversity of craft.

Take socks as a microcosm: in her book *Folk Socks,* Nancy Bush explores the history (and prehistory) of knitted foot coverings, and then gives examples from more than a dozen countries. In her turn, Priscilla Gibson-Roberts fills *Ethnic Socks and Stockings* with twenty-six more examples—with almost no overlap. Not to slight those who go for depth rather than breadth, let me also recommend Anna Zilboorg's comprehensive tome on Turkish socks, *Fancy Feet.* Bet you didn't know that traditional Turkish socks have different patterns on the sole than they do on the leg and instep! Very sensible in a world where shoes are removed upon entering the house, and people sit on cushions on the floor—friends and family see the bottom of your socks.

Until the last decade or so, knitting in the United States mostly followed its own generic, fashion-driven path: knitting magazines from the 1930s photographed models to look like movie stars, and patterns in *Women's Day* boasted that they were modeled after styles right off the Paris runways. My grandmother and her sister knitted tailored suits with jackets that featured dressmaking details like lapel facings and belts. *Vogue Knitting* still provides instructions for knitted bikini bathing suits and other garments copied from ready-to-wear.

Only a few folk-knitting traditions penetrated the American knitter's consciousness from the 1960s to the '80s: Aran, or fisherman's, sweaters, with their characteristic cable designs; Shetland sweaters in the style of Fair Isle—usually plain pullovers with a band of OXO patterning in heathery colors at the yoke; Icelandic "ski sweaters," bulky garments of unspun roving yarn, often in undyed shades of gray and brown, with bold geometric patterns at the yoke. The first two were probably brought to our attention by tourists coming back from the British Isles with souvenirs; the third was helped by Reynolds Yarn Company's introduction of the traditional Lopi yarn (and patterns to go with it).

And there were dissenting voices—Elizabeth Zimmerman's instructions in *Vogue Knitting* in 1957 for an Aran sweater, with information on how to design one's own; Priscilla Gibson-Roberts's 1985 book *Knitting in the Old Way*, which covered numerous ethnic traditions for garment shaping and construction. But for the most part, American knitting stayed turned in on itself until the late 1980s.

Since then, however, our eyes have been opened to the wealth of world knitting traditions by a seemingly endless procession of new books attempting to document and preserve local knitting ways. In *Latvian Mittens*, Lizbeth Upitis shows mittens in an incredibly rich cultural context. Latvian mittens are elaborately patterned, covered with geometric and floral motifs in brilliant colors and fine-gauge yarns. They are given as gifts for many social occasions, especially rites of passage: a bride might knit fifty pairs of mittens in preparation for her wedding day, and need them all. She'd give a pair to the man who drove the wagon to take her to the church, a pair to the groom, a pair to both her new mother- and father-in-law, and so on through the day. When she and her new husband reached her new home, she would hang pairs of mittens over the barn door (to promote fertility among the cattle) and in the orchard (to ensure a good harvest).

Latvian Mittens gives extensive photos of mittens, each identified by the village where it was made, and the text is in both English and Latvian. Thus it provides a glimpse of a distant world to American knitters, but also encyclopedic documentation for Latvians of their own artifacts. As in so many other places, the old ways are dwindling away in Lativa. Upitis's book is a permanent record as well as an introduction for outsiders.

In neighboring Estonia, Nancy Bush attended a conference about knitting and visited the national museum as part of her research for *Folk Knitting in Estonia.* She writes that "it is important for knitters to know their roots, so to speak, to understand something about the landscape and the culture that created the environment for designs to evolve, to have a sense of where the inspiration originated."

In *Andean Folk Knitting: Traditions and Techniques from Peru and Bolivia,* Cynthia Gravelle le Count describes a similar anthropological mission. She was struck by the beautiful knitwear she saw in the region when she visited for other research, and she realized that "in many areas traditional dress was worn less frequently . . . . There was obviously a need to preserve examples of knitted ethnic clothing and accessories and to document their cultural context." She traces not only the different patterns associated with different regions, but the gender roles involved: in Peru and Bolivia, knitting is predominantly men's work. Boys of ten make their own ch'ullus, the distinctive pointed cap with earflaps; by the time they are adolescents, they are very skilled and improvise their own colors and patterning. Interestingly, in a region where men no longer wear the traditional ch'ullu, "mothers spin and dye the sheep's wool they use to knit colorful little caps for their baby boys and girls." Women do customarily knit sweaters and socks for their families, and also for sale to tourists in some regions.

The mother-daughter team of Biddy and Annie Hurlbut found these highly qualified knitters in the late 1970s and began the design and import business now known as Peruvian Connection. The first sweaters were in the natural browns and grays of undyed alpaca; they now have a palette of more than one hundred twenty colors. For their Spring 2001 catalog, they introduced new designs by Kaffe Fassett (who worked with English knitters to produce ready-to-wear before his knitting patterns began to be published).

There are, of course, beautiful books that exist primarily as pattern resources. The introduction to *Mostly Mittens* discusses the Komi people (an ethnic group living in northeastern Russia, just west of the Ural mountains) and the influences of Latvian and Estonian knitting motifs on Komi designs. Most of the book, however, is devoted to beautiful mittens (and a few hats and socks!) in Komi patterns. The instructions are for widely available yarns and require knitters to work at small but not unheard-of gauges: author Charlene Schurch has adapted the patterns and worked out the technical details for us.

This is a serious job for those interested in ethnic textiles, which present multiple challenges. First, precisely because they were produced by folk traditions, there are no formal written instructions or standard sizes. Knitters do what they have always done, as they were taught by the previous generation of knitters, and they improvise changes to custom-fit their family members. Second, much ethnic knitting is done at gauges that would stagger American knitters. Latvian mittens routinely have ten to twelve stitches per inch. The fine gauge allows for fantastic pattern detail, as well as fabric that is thin and flexible enough to wear for work. Few contemporary urban knitters would attempt such things, even for a relatively small project like mittens or socks. The challenge for authors such as Bush, Upitis, and Schurch is to produce patterns that are as authentic as possible while making them useful to their intended audience (who would be hard put even to find yarns thin enough for the original).

Not all of these books are produced by outsiders. Henriette C. van der Klift-Tellegen explains the impulse behind her book, *Knitting from the Netherlands: Traditional Dutch Fishermen's Sweaters,* as an outgrowth of the broader trend: "During the past ten years there has been a growing interest in traditional sweaters from other countries." This led her to look for indigenous sweaters in her native Holland. When she began her research, she found that the traditional sweaters were "nearly extinct . . . . If these designs are to be preserved, speed is of the essence." She does the job admirably, providing information on sweaters from twenty-one different villages. For each village, she includes a photograph of at least one man in an exemplary sweater, plus charts for the characteristic stitches and notes on pattern layout and sizing.

Some untranslated works can be almost as useful. The three volumes of *Überlieferte Strickmuster aus dem Steirischen Ennstal (Traditional Knitting Patterns from the Styrian Enns River Valley)* each contain more than fifty stitch patterns plus examples of stockings and sweaters with instructions—all in German. But the stitches are so clearly photographed, and the accompanying charts use such a small set of fairly simple symbols, that most knitters only need a brief glossary of the symbols to use the patterns. (Fortunately, Schoolhouse Press, the U.S. distributor of the books, has included such a glossary.) Styria is a province of Austria, and the knitting patterns traditional there use travelling stitches—like tiny one-stitch cables crossing over one another in elaborate ropes, knots, and lattices. Contemporary knitters might not make any of the fine-gauge, densely patterned knee-high stockings exactly as shown (perfect with lederhosen!), but those in search of a unique cable panel for the center of a sweater or scarf will find endless inspiration here.

Japanese knitting patterns (yes, there's knitting in Japan) are usable by knitters everywhere, because they use almost no words at all. Instead, a large schematic diagram of the garment has symbols and numbers at key points. For instance, if the sweater begins at the bottom edge, there will be a note at the bottom of the diagram that says something like "(1) 50-60-70 sts ↑ " to indicate that one begins by casting on 50 stitches for the smallest size, 60 for the medium, etc., and proceeds to knit upward. The next note might appear at the underarm and say, "(2) 20-22-24 cm b.o. 5-5-5 decr E2R 3-4-5," and a knitter making the smallest size would know to bind off 5 stitches at each side when the piece measured 20 centimeters, and then to decrease 1 stitch at each end of every second row 3 times. If the sweater has a stitch pattern, it usually appears in a chart off to the side, along with information about gauge, yarn requirements, etc. Here again, an American knitter with a glossary to show that the symbol "日" means "stitches" is pretty much ready to go. (Where to find such a key? Look for the book *Knitting Languages,* or a copy of *Knitters* magazine from Spring 1997, which included a terrific article on the topic.) Another benefit of the Japanese system is efficiency: almost every sweater fits on one page. Moreover, one can see at a glance where the shaping is done in case changes are needed for fit.

Are you beginning to get the feeling that you can find knitting all over the world? You can go a step further: you can find knitted *mittens* all over the world. *Folk Mittens,* by Marcia Lewandowski, offers thirty-eight different mitten patterns from some nineteen countries, discussing the fiber and handcovering traditions of each area as well as indigenous knitting techniques. Along with *Latvian Mittens* and *Mostly Mittens, The Mitten Book* by Inger and Ingrid G. Gottfridsson concentrates on mittens from one area only—in this case, Gotland, an island off the southeast coast of Sweden.

As goods and services migrate around the world, knitters get the benefit of modern innovation as well. Dale of Norway is a yarn company that's been making Heilo, a very durable sport-weight wool, for more than sixty years. Since 1956, Dale has also been responsible for designing an official sweater for the Norwegian national ski team each year. The designs are usually traditional, featuring highly symmetrical geometric and snowflake motifs, usually in white or off-white on a navy or black background (though in recent years there have been many alternate colorways featuring brighter blues, rust, and green). In Norway, the ski team members are celebrities, and people knit and wear the sweaters to show support for the team, so the patterns are sized for every member of the family, starting with infants.

The importation of the yarns and patterns into the United States in the mid-1980s introduced American knitters to entirely new construction techniques. Nordic sweaters are knit in the round, in continuous tubes all the way to the shoulder, and then armholes are cut into the body and sleeves sewn in. For cardigans, the main tube is cut all the way from top to bottom as well. The elaborate color patterns are much easier to knit this way, and the Dale sweaters feature knitted facings at the top of the sleeve and the neck edges that cover the cut edges with a beautiful finish. The modern innovation in all this? Before cutting into the body, one uses a sewing machine to reinforce the edges—an unnecessary step, but reassuring to novices.

The annual ski-team sweater from Dale is not the only kind of Norwegian knitting available in the United States, either. The design team of Tone Takle and Lise Kolstad has written three books—*Sweaters, More Sweaters,* and *Small Sweaters*—all of which have been translated into English and distributed here. While they use the same techniques for knitting in the round and cutting where necessary, their aesthetic is entirely different. Their sweaters feature bold, bright colors in strong floral designs, often with multiple patterns of different scale playing off one another within a single garment. Garment shapes, too, are far from traditional: boxy pullovers are rare, replaced by tunics, leggings, coats, dolman sleeves, and hats in a variety of shapes to stagger the imagination. One typical outfit for little girls features a tunic in red with pink tulips with details in bright green and yellow and a ruffled edge, plus tights striped in the same colors and a matching striped hat that is somehow a cross between a large beret and a long stocking cap. What a wonderful way to brighten dark winter days!

Some knitting traditions have been preserved by the buying power of American knitters. Galina Khmeleva found the knitters of the Orenburg region of Russia earning a meager subsistence for their ravishing shawls and scarves, and began bringing the pieces to America to sell. The lacy garments are made of a two-ply yarn processed by the knitters themselves in their homes: one ply is incredibly fine mohair from goats raised in the village (often, in the knitter's backyard), the other, commercially-spun silk. The knitters harvest and spin the mohair, wind both it and the silk on separate disk-shaped bobbins, and then knit with both together. Shawls may be natural white or various shades of brown and gray. Khmeleva has also written a book illustrating the traditional construction techniques and the various pattern elements of the shawls, and she travels the United States teaching workshops. She brings shawls with her to sell, because she has found that knitters who are learning to make their own will often also buy completed shawls. We appreciate the workmanship more than anyone else!

Wendy Keele's book, *Poems of Color*, documents Swedish Bohus knitting. This style was a cottage industry in the mid-twentieth century. The designs were developed and the knitters organized in the late 1930s by Emma Jacobsson, who came to the area as a bride and wanted to help local women survive in the depressed economy. The angora sweaters (and hats and mittens) were sold in upscale department stores and, after World War II, to European and American tourists. Keele's 1995 book examines careers of individual designers as well as providing complete instructions for plenty of sweaters. The patterns combine knit/purl textures with small-repeat geometric patterns in many shades of color; the results are luxurious, rich, subtle, and complex.

Contemporary knitters have ready access to appropriate yarns for a global variety of knits as well. We take the availability of Lopi yarn for granted, but we also have Shetland wools from Scottish mills and traditional gansey yarns from England. We do not stop to think about the number of different types of fiber we use, but the local yarn shop represents a worldwide menagerie. Close examination of any shelf will reveal the global economy at work. The pure cashmere we stocked for a recent Fall season came from an Italian maker, distributed by a company in Massachusetts, spun of fiber harvested from animals in Asia. When a Michigan distributor offers us alpaca under a French label, the fine print shows that, like almost all alpaca, it came from animals in South America: every fiber in the skein has crossed the Atlantic twice by the time it reaches us. Even our basic synthetic-based afghan yarn is spun in Turkey. We have wool from Australia, New Zealand, Japan, Norway, England, Scotland, Wales, France, Germany, Italy, Switzerland, Canada, the United States, and Uruguay. Our cottons come from England, Norway, Italy, Belgium, Germany, Greece, and Peru, plus one that's grown and spun in the United States, then dyed in Canada. When I get phone calls asking if we carry "imported" yarn, I have to laugh, but the answer is easy. The problem is knowing what constitutes a *domestic* yarn if anyone wants one.

If I say that these books and resources offer a way to explore the world through knitting, you know I mean as an armchair traveler. But you can literally explore the world through knitting: there are lots of opportunities for knitting-related travel.

Knitters magazine produces some of the best-known domestic knitting events, Stitches and Camp Stitches. Stitches is a three-day knitting extravaganza, featuring dozens of classes and a market-place with hundreds of vendors. The classes range from introductory-level to expert and are taught by instructors, designers, and authors from all over the country. You can learn how to make jewelry by knitting with wire, or five different ways to cast on, or how to design a sweater. I once took an all-day class with a woman named Susie Hodges who taught us all how to knit two-color patterns holding one strand of yarn in each hand. The class changed my knitting life, both because of Susie's techniques and because of what I learned about knitting in the round from my fellow students.

When the class was over, I went downstairs to the marketplace, which was in the main exhibition hall of the convention center where Stitches was held. There were aisle after aisle of booths—people were selling handspun, hand-dyed yarns; bags of close-out and discontinued yarn at incredibly low prices; specialty yarns spun from specific breeds of wool; books; patterns; handmade needles; tote bags; antique buttons; handmade fused-glass buttons; hand-made polymer-clay buttons; wooden buttons dyed to match specific yarns; buttons made from the shed antlers of reindeer . . . . And there were demonstrations on the show floor, of how to use knitting machines or knitting software or how to knit scarves from unspun silk "caps" called *mawata*.

I found a booth from a place called Viking Design where the proprietor, Sandy Terp, had tiny rolls of fine silk/wool in an apparently endless variety of colors; six or eight were strung together on a cord for some ridiculous price like five dollars. I bought two sets in shades of blue and green. At home, I used a 16-inch circular needle in size 2 and cast on 160 stitches with the silk. I had found a used copy of Alice Starmore's *Book of Fair Isle Knitting* and I began practicing the techniques from class, using patterns from the book's "Pattern Library" chapter.

I worked on the scarf off and on for months; the small gauge made it the kind of thing one has to be awake and alert to knit, and some nights I just didn't have what it took. The next summer, I began to worry that I was running out of some of the best colors. I wrote to Sandy Terp and enclosed snips of the yarn (which turned out to be Zephyr, from Jaggerspun in Springvale, Maine). She replied that some of the colors were discontinued, but she sent me some similar ones. As Stitches began to come around again, I thought a little about how long the scarf should finally be. Ultimately, I stayed up all night and finally bound off at about six in the morning. I flattened my tube of scarf and sewed the cast-on and bound-off edges shut (this way all the ends from where I had joined new colors were hidden forever on the inside). I went to Stitches again and found Susie Hodges to show her what I'd done with the class. The scarf is about 40 inches long and, at 8 inches wide, was knit at a gauge of about 10 stitches to the inch. Of all the things I've knitted, it's probably the one of which I'm proudest.

Stitches takes place three times each year: in February in California; in August in the Midwest; and in October on the East Coast (usually Valley Forge, Pennsylvania). Information is always available through *Knitters*.

Camp Stitches is organized more around classes, with dozens (rather than thousands) of participants altogether. It is held in a lakeside resort in upstate New York in June. Pictures show people on long porches knitting in Adirondack chairs (there's no need to tote massive bags from convention floor to parking lot). The tone is still one of enormous energy and excitement, but the setting is bucolic.

Not to be outdone, *Vogue Knitting* and *Interweave Knits* have begun organizing knitting tours. These ten-day to two-week adventures to fiber-rich destinations such as Scandinavia or the United Kingdom feature visits to mills and museums and workshops with such renowned designers as Sasha Kagan and Alice Starmore. *Vogue* has also offered a cruise to Alaska featuring shipboard classes with the likes of Kaffe Fassett and Nicky Epstein.

Such expeditions provide two kinds of opportunity to connect with other knitters: one's fellow travelers, and the hosts or "natives" along the way. The possibilities for cultural exchange are boundless and invigorating. Three miles from home in the library, or 3,000 miles from home on a sheep farm, you too can be knitting in the global village.

PROJECT: *Multi-Cultural Mittens*

Here's a pair of mittens that makes the most of the enormous variety of fibers and techniques we have literally at our finger-tips. One of the yarns is a pure alpaca, grown and spun in Peru for a yarn company in Lowell, Massachusetts. (Lucy Larcom and her fellow millworkers are long gone, but there are still quite a lot of yarn companies in western Mass.) The other is merino wool, grown and spun in Canada for Maie and Taiu Landra, a mother-daughter team born in Estonia who hand-paint it in uniquely beautiful ways. The cuff is an all-purpose rib common all over Western Europe; the thumb gusset is typical of Norway; the top shaping could come from anywhere in Scandinavia. The color pattern is a variation on a Komi design from Mostly Mittens.

Size: Women's Medium

Materials: 2 sk Classic Elite "Inca" color 1108 dark brown (A)

  1 sk Koigu Painter's Palette Premium Merino color 314 brown mix (B)

  Size 3 dpn, or size to obtain gauge

  stitch holder

  2 ring markers

Gauge: 7½ sts = 1" over stockinette st

Left Mitten
Cuff:

Using A, cast on 52 sts. Work in k2, p2 rib for 2½", incr to 60 sts on last rnd. Hand: Change to stockinette and work color patt from chart twice for each round. Work through Rnd 20. Est thumb gusset:

Work 22 sts in patt from chart, place marker, m1 with color A, k1A, m1A, place marker; beg with st 24 on chart, work to end of rnd. Next rnd: Work sts 1 through 22 from chart, slip marker, m1A, k2A, k1B, m1A, slip marker, work from st 24 to end of rnd according to chart. Cont to work sts 1–22 before gusset and sts 24–30 and 1–30 after gusset while working gusset sts as follows: **Rnd 22:** M1A, k2A, k3B, m1A. **Rnd 23:** M1A, k2A, k3B, k2A, m1A. **Rnd 24:** M1A, k2A, k3B, k3A, k1B, m1A. **Rnd 25:** M1A, k2A, k3B, k3A, k3B, m1A. **Rnd 26:** M1A, k2A, k3B, k3A, k3B, k2A, m1A. **Rnd 27:** M1A, k2A, (k3B, k3A) twice, k1B, m1A. **Rnd 28:** M1A, k2A, (k3B, k3A) twice, k3B, m1A. **Next rnd:** Work 22 sts, cast on 1 st, remove marker, slip 19 gusset sts to holder, remove 2nd marker, k to end of rnd.

Cont with chart to end of rnd 54. Begin top decreases: *k1A, ssk with A, work through st 28, k2togA; rep from *.

Rnd 56: *k1A, sskA, work through st 27, k2tog A; rep from *.

■ A
□ B

Cont to decr 4 sts on each rnd as established through rnd 67 (8 sts rem). Cut yarn, leaving a 6" tail. Thread through rem sts, draw tight, secure end.

Right mitten:

Work as for Left Mitten, est thumb gusset on Rnd 20 by working 37 sts before placing 1st marker and 22 sts after 2nd.

Thumb:

Place 19 sts from holder on 2 ndls. With 3rd ndl and A, pick up and k 5 sts along edge of hole on hand.

Rnd 1: K2A, (k3B, k3A) 3 times, k3B, k1A. **Rnd 2:** K1A, (k3B, k3A) 3 times, k3B, k2A. **Rnd 3:** (K3B, k3A) 4 times. **Rnd 4:** K2B, (k3A, k3B) 3 times, k3A, k1B. **Rnd 5:** K1B, (k3A, k3B) 3 times, k3A, k2B. **Rnd 6:** (K3A, k3B) 4 times. Rep these 6 rnds until thumb meas 2" from picked-up sts (or desired length to tip). Cut B. With A, (k1, k2tog) around. **Next rnd:** K2tog around—8 sts rem. Cut yarn, draw through rem sts, fasten off. Weave in ends.

Knitting to Improve the World

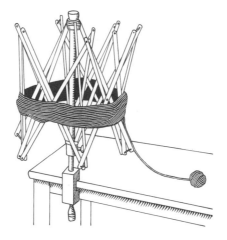

S ome would argue that the very act of knitting improves the world: that regardless of what one knits or for whom, one increases the amount of good in the world by doing something slowly and with care. Despite our society's constant drive for greater speed and "efficiency," a knitter has deliberately chosen to keep an old craft from dying out and fading away. And I can guarantee that anyone who's ever worn a cozy, soft, handknit hat during a snowstorm will tell you that knitters improve the world.

For knitters who want to go further, though, and make a more public difference, there are literally hundreds of ways to use your knitting to improve the world. This chapter will look at some of them.

Perhaps the most obvious is "charity" knitting: you knit a garment and give it to someone in need. In doing so, you fulfill the biblical precept to clothe the needy. You could also do this by writing a check to a service organization or donating old clothes, but you go a step further. The recipient feels warmed by more than the fabric when the garment is hand-knit. Popular projects for this kind of work are small but high-impact: hats, scarves, squares for afghans. For example, many hospitals are happy to receive knit caps for premature babies (whose heads are too small for commercially available ones, but who have even more trouble keeping warm than full-term newborns). If you ask at your local hospital, you may find that a group is already active. But do not worry if there isn't one. Start doing the work yourself. You needn't commit to providing a hat for every preemie in the nursery; just make a hat or two when you feel like it, and mention what you are doing to your friends. Be sure to use a non-allergenic, easy-care yarn for this and all items to be donated. You will find instructions for a cap at the end of this chapter (see page 155).

If you like to make slightly larger hats, contact your local children's hospital and see if they would welcome hats for kids who lose their hair as a result of chemotherapy. For these, use a regular child's hat pattern; think bright, cheerful colors, and remember, nothing itchy!

Two blanket projects merit special mention. One is Project Linus, which provides blankets to young children with serious illnesses. (Contact information for Project Linus and other organizations mentioned in this chapter can be found in "Resources" (see page 162).

Warm Up America! provides full-size afghans to shelters across the country. The prospect of knitting an entire afghan for charity may be daunting—but don't worry. Warm Up America! has broken the job down into squares (rectangles, actually). Participants knit 9- x 7-inch blocks, which are then assembled into afghans. You can use any color, any stitch you like—just make sure your block is the right size. This is a great opportunity to try out a new stitch. Or take this as the impetus to knit a nice large gauge swatch for your next project. It will not be wasted; you will use it in an afghan. The organization would prefer that you accumulate the requisite 49 squares and assemble the blanket locally, then send it to them for distribution. Ask around at local yarn stores; some collect squares, and then have assembly parties to complete and send the afghan.

If your favorite charities do not lend themselves to donations of knitted goods, you can knit to raise cash. Many knitters I know donate knitted items to charity auctions for local schools or AIDS service organizations. For school groups, it is easy to choose a simple child's sweater or hat in the school colors. For adult audiences, a pair of thick socks or a cushy scarf has lots of appeal without taking too much time or yarn. When the organizers need to know the value of an item to be auctioned, do not underestimate. Use the retail price of the yarn (even if it was in your stash), and calculate the value of your labor. Not everyone who considers bidding will be familiar with handknit goods, and you must educate them. They don't know how comfortable those socks are and they do not know that they cannot just go out and buy such amazing socks.

Maybe the biggest knitting fundraiser of this sort is A Bear in Sheep's Clothing, founded and run by Judith Shangold. Her work as a sales rep didn't fulfill her need to do some good in the world; in her spare time she volunteered with an AIDS hotline. In 1991 she found a way to combine her career with her altruistic work. She approached prominent designers of handknits such as Deborah Newton, Nicky Epstein, and Elizabeth Zimmerman, and asked each to produce a knitted outfit for a teddy bear which would then be auctioned for charity.

Every one of the eighteen designers she approached agreed.

The bears were featured in a special "Kids" issue of *Vogue Knitting,* with patterns for complementary children's sweaters. Instructions for making the bears' clothing were published in a separate booklet, sales of which also went to charity. In all, the project generated $32,000 for the Children's Aid Society that year. Judith also accepted contributions of dressed bears from private knitters which would then be sold at bazaars and craft shows. Over the years, various women's and children's charities have benefited. Though she no longer distributes the stuffed bears, Judith still donates money from the sale of pattern booklets.

It wouldn't be difficult to launch one's own version of this project: bear clothes are *small,* which means they use very little yarn and are quick to make. Lots of cute patterns are available through A Bear in Sheep's Clothing, and they are already sized for commonly available bears. With a couple of knitting friends and a couple months of preparation, one could have a table full of unique, adorable bears at a church bazaar. Post a sign indicating that sales support a good cause, and watch the bears go. For more ideas, see *Spin-Off* magazine from Spring 1996, which has dressed bears on the cover as well as in a feature story inside.

Judith Shangold is also the owner of Design Source, the U.S. distributor of Manos del Uruguay yarns. The story of Manos del Uruguay is a classic tale of knitting to improve the world. In 1967, a hepatitis epidemic in the mountains of Uruguay brought many people from the countryside into the larger villages for medical care. While they were there, some of the women were taught to knit by some volunteers who were also organizing activities for the children. Through the years, the women have organized themselves into several cooperatives and begun spinning and dyeing their own yarn from local Merino and Corriedale fleece. Handknitted sweaters and woven goods are now available from shops in Montevideo and are exported to Japan and several countries in North and South America and Europe; yarn comes to the United States. The cooperatives provide work for about 400 women in a very depressed area where opportunities are few. Recall the insight from Barber's *Women's Work:* this is work that even mothers of small children can do at home.

And the yarn itself is beautiful: it's a chunky single-ply that knits at about 3½ to 4 stitches to the inch on a U.S. size 8 or 9 needle. Because it is Merino and Corriedale, and because it's a softly-spun single, it is soft enough for many people to wear next to the skin. The handspun quality produces gentle variations in thickness. The colors have variations, too, because they're kettle-dyed in small batches. Within each skein, color can vary in lightness and/or brightness, and from batch to batch many of the colors differ tremendously. ("Stone," for instance, can be a light brown-gray with streaks of pink—or it can be an almost solid gray-green.) There are 72 colors available, from strong brights to incredibly subtle neutrals with names like Briar and Oilslick. In addition, there are 13 multicolors, truly variegated combinations like Woodland, which has scarlet, tangerine, and olive green, plus all of their lighter and darker shades.

No, Manos isn't inexpensive, but there are a lot of more expensive yarns on the market, and no one who uses Manos regrets it, in my experience. It has been said that if you start a new knitter on Manos for her first project, she'll be a knitter for life. It's that much of a pleasure to knit with. Moreover, when you knit with Manos, you know that you are improving the quality of life for women and their children a continent away.

A responsible consumer—someone who thinks about how things are made, and where the money goes, and what kind of practices she wants to support—has a lot of opportunities to improve the world with her knitting. Here are a few other fiber sources to consider:

Sally Fox has developed a line of cotton yarn called Fox Fibre that comes in colors but is not dyed—selective breeding has yielded several shades of gold and brown, plus a green. The color does not fade over time or with exposure to light; in fact, it deepens with repeated washings. Undyed fibers are much easier on the environment than dyed ones; for more information, see the Fox Fibre Web site (see Resources, page 162). Fox Fibre is available as handknitting yarn through the site as well.

Shetland 2000 is undyed wool in nine shades of ivory, brown, and gray. It has all the benefits of undyed yarn, plus more: it is made from the fleece of Shetland sheep, a breed known for the fineness and softness of its wool. Shetland 2000 is a Save the Sheep project, meaning that it seeks to preserve and promote the rare Shetland breed. (Demand for bright-white fleece, which takes dye well, has caused other breeds to be imported to replace the native breed with its many natural colors.) The goal is to prevent extinction of a breed, but also of a lifestyle: not much grows in the harsh environment of the tiny Shetland islands, and young people must increasingly leave the islands for cities on the Scottish mainland to find work. By promoting use of the wool in the United States (pattern support for Shetland 2000 is excellent—there are ravishing, subtle, modern multicolored designs by Ron Schweitzer, and at least one beautiful cabled tunic by Anna Zilboorg), the company hopes to maintain demand at a level that will allow the mill to stay in operation. Betty Lindsay, co-owner of Shetland 2000, quotes her husband as saying, "'You can't save the economy of Shetland single-handedly,' and I just tell him, 'I don't have to. I've got all these lovely knitters to help me.'"

Peace Fleece was founded in the 1980s to promote "U.S.-Soviet cooperation." It imported wool from the USSR and combined it with wool from the United States to produce a heavy worsted-weight yarn in a lovely palette of soft, heathery shades. The fall of the Soviet Union did not mean the end of the company or the project, though. If anything, Russia needs economic opportunities more now than it used to, and Peace Fleece is still available. The company also imports knitting needles from Russia; they have red beads at the top handpainted with charming folk-art designs. See their Web site for information (see Resources, page 162) about their ongoing work with Jewish and Arab sheep farmers in Israel.

Finally, many people use knitting to improve the world by teaching more people to knit. I know a woman who worked as a counselor at a drop-in center for recovering drug addicts. She got donations of yarn and supplies and began teaching her clients to knit—she said it was good for them to have something to do with their hands, and to learn to do something with clear, immediate results. She called it her own needle-exchange program.

People who teach children to knit report all kinds of benefits. Phyllis Rodgers-Young worked with fifth graders in the Philadelphia public schools and reported that after a semester of practice, the classroom teacher found that the students' handwriting had improved. Lisa Scarpello teaches first- through third-grade children at an after-school program in a private school; the children make garter-stitch squares which can then be variously tied, sewn, and stuffed to resemble animals. Parents have told her supervisor that they have to rearrange their child's other extracurricular activities because the kid is determined not to miss knitting!

Taking a page from Waldorf schools, which have always made knitting a part of the curriculum from first grade through sixth, Debbie Bakan teaches all of her first-grade class at a Philadelphia-area Friends school to knit. The project began with one child who was begging to learn, and spread as Debbie enlisted each new knitter to teach another. The children now knit blocks for afghans to be donated to Warm Up America! as part of their service learning. They do the necessary gauge calcuations to make the blocks come out the right size—pretty sophisticated math for six- and seven-year-olds. Some of the assembly of the blocks is done at home as a way of encouraging family involvement. Among the other benefits Debbie has seen are increased fine motor control, increased ability to organize and plan, and improved ability to go back and fix errors.

If you've gotten to this point in this book, you know the benefits of knitting to the adult knitter. To summarize briefly: the process brings calm, peace, an opportunity for contemplation, a sense of purpose and utility, and pure visual and tactile pleasure. The product brings custom wardrobe items, precious gifts, and a sense of achievement and self-confidence. Knitting can become the lens through which you see the world and its many important issues—politics, economics, gender relations, travel. In our career-driven age, you can choose to define yourself as a knitter rather than as a lawyer, a physical therapist, a bank teller. You are the recipient and conduit of an old and precious craft. If you teach someone else to knit, you open this world to her.

My charge to you is twofold: first, if you can, find the person who taught you to knit, and thank her or him. Second, find someone who doesn't know how to knit, and pass on the gift.

PROJECT:
Watch Cap for Preemies

This is an awfully small version of the hat from Chapter 7 (see page 87).

Size: to fit head circumference of 8–9"

Materials: less than 50 yds of DK-weight acrylic baby yarn, such as Wendy "Peter Pan DK"

 Size 5 dpn, or size to obtain
   gauge

Gauge: as much as 8 sts = 1" over rib when relaxed; as little as 4 sts = 1" over rib when stretched

Hat:

Cast on 48 sts. Work in k2, p2 rib for 5¼". Shape top: (K2, p2tog) around (36 sts). Next rnd: (K2tog, p1) around (24 sts). Next rnd: K2tog around. Rep last rnd once: 6 sts rem. Cut yarn, draw through rem sts, fasten off. Weave in ends. Fold cuff up 1".

Knitting Basics

Long-Tail Cast-On

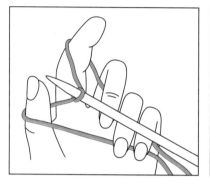

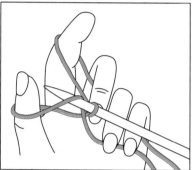

1. Make a slip knot and place on right needle. Put left thumb and forefinger between strands and into "slingshot" position.

2. Bring needle under strand at base of thumb (from outside) and up . . .

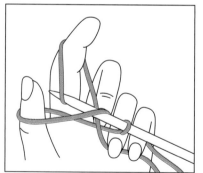

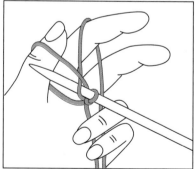

3. . . . over strand at forefinger, then back down . . .

4. . . . under thumb strand and out toward your body. Drop strand from thumb and tighten new stitch.

Basic Knit Stitch

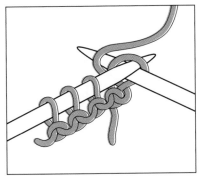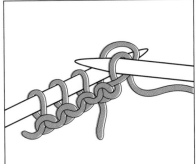

1. Insert right needle through stitch from front to back. Wrap yarn counter-clockwise around tip of right needle.

2. Pull needle back through stitch to the front, keeping wrap on needle.

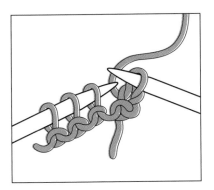

3. Slide old stitch off tip of left needle. Repeat from Step 1.

Basic Purl Stitch

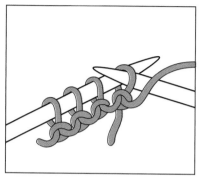 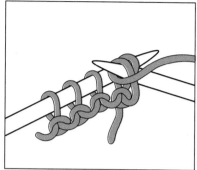

1. Insert right needle through stitch from back to front.

2. Wrap yarn counter-clockwise around tip of needle. Pull needle back through stitch to back of work, keeping wrap on needle.

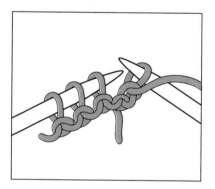

3. Slide old stitch off tip of left needle. Repeat from Step 1.

Double-Point Needles

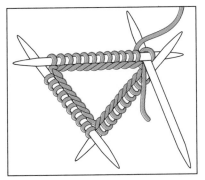

Picking Up Stitches

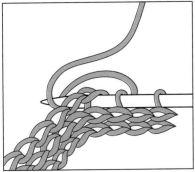

Cast on stitches on one needle, then slide one-third of them onto each of two other needles. Arrange needles into triangle as shown, being careful not to let stitches twist around needles. Pick up a fourth needle in your right hand; use this to knit the stitches from the first needle. When the first needle is empty, move it to your right hand and use it to knit the stitches from the second needle—and so on around.

Starting at right-hand edge and looking at the right side of the work, insert the right needle through the fabric from front to back (make sure to be at least 2 threads in from the edge, i.e. between the first and second stitches of the row). Wrap the yarn around the needle as if to knit. Pull wrap back through fabric to form new stitch.

Knit Grafting

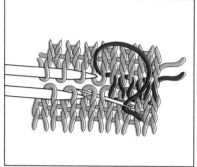

Lifted-Strand Increase

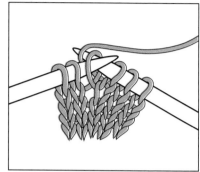

Thread yarn through darning needle; go in and out through the "live" stitches, tracing the path of an imaginary row of stitches between them.

With the point of the left needle, go under the strand that runs between the last stitch and the next one. Knit into the back of the strand to twist it.

Knitting Abbreviations

alt	alternate	psso	pass slipped stitch over
approx	approximately	pwise	purlwise, as if to purl
b	bobble	rem	remaining
bc	back cross	rep	repeat
beg	beginning	rev stst	reverse stockinette stitch
bo	bind off	RS	right side
cc	contrasting color	rnd(s)	round(s)
cm	centimeter(s)	sk	skein
cn	cable needle	skp	slip one, knit one, pass
co	cast on		slipped stitch over
cont	continue	sl	slip
dec	decrease, decreasing	ssk	slip, slip, knit (slip 2 sts
dpn	double-pointed needle(s)		one at a time knitwise
foll	following		from left ndl to right;
g	grams		insert point of left ndl
inc	increase, increasing		back onto both sts and
k	knit		k2tog)
kbl, ktbl	knit through back of loop	st(s)	stitch(es)
k2tog	knit 2 together	stst	stockinette (or stocking)
kwise	knitwise, as if to knit		stitch
lh	left hand	tbl	through back of loop
m	meter(s)	tog	together
m1	make one	WS	wrong side
mb	make bobble	wyib	with yarn in back
mc	main color	wyif	with yarn in front
meas	measure	yf	yarn forward
ndl	needle(s)	yo	yarn over
opp	opposite	yo2	yarn over twice
oz	ounce(s)	*	repeat instructions as
p	purl		often as indicated
p2tog	purl 2 together	[ ]	repeat instructions inside
patt	pattern		brackets as often as
pm	place marker		indicated

Resources

The Knitting Guild of America
2692 Richmond Rd., Ste. 205
Lexington, KY 40509
(800) 969-6069
www.tkga.com

Charitable
Design Source
(888) 566-9970
shangold@usa.net

Project Linus
P. O. Box 5621
Bloomington, IL 61702-5621
www.projectlinus.org

Warm Up America!
2500 Lowell Rd.
Gastonia, NC 28054
www.craftyarncouncil.com/
warmup.html

For more information on
knitting for charitable causes:
Carlin's Knitting Page
www.math.vanderbilt.edu/~cjs/
knitting.html

Computer
The Knitting Universe
www.knittinguniverse.com

Woolworks
www.woolworks.org

www.knitting.about.com

Knitlist
www.kniton.com

Fibers
Shetland 2000
www.yarnsinternational.com
www.shetland-wool-
brokers.zetnet.co.uk/
shet2000.htm

Fox Fibre
www.foxfibre.com

Peace Fleece
www.peacefleece.com

Design Source
shangold@usa.net
(888) 566-9970

Mission Falls 1824 wool
Unique Kolours
(800) 252-DYE4

Wendy Peter Pan DK
Berroco Yarns
(800) 343-4948

Classic Elite Yarns
(800) 343-0308

Rowan Yarns
Westminster Fibers
(800) 445-9276

Mountain Colors
(406) 777-3377

Koigu Wool Designs
(519) 794-3066
www.koigu.com

Bibliography

Barber, Elizabeth Wayland. *Women's Work: The First 20,000 Years: Women, Cloth, and Society in Early Times.* New York: Norton, 1994.

Brown-Reinsel, Beth: *Knitting Ganseys.* Loveland, Colo.: Interweave Press, 1993.

Buller, Kate. *The Ultimate Knitter's Guide.* Bothell, Wash.: Martingale & Co., 2000.

Bush, Nancy. *Folk Knitting in Estonia: A Garland of Symbolism, Tradition, and Technique.* Loveland, Colo.: Interweave Press, 1999.

— *Folk Socks: The History and Techniques of Handknitted Footwear.* Loveland, Colo.: Interweave Press, 1994.

Dickinson, Emily. *The Complete Poems of Emily Dickinson.* Cambridge, Mass.: The Belknap Press of Harvard University Press, 1979.

Erlbacher, Maria. *Uberlieferte Strickmuster aus dem Steirischen Ennstal.*Trautenfels, 1986.

Fassett, Kaffe. *Glorious Color for Needlepoint and Knitting.* New York: Sterling, 1993.

— *Glorious Knitting.* New York: C. N. Potter, 1985.

— and Zoe Hunt. *Family Album: More Glorious Knits for Children and Adults.* New York: C. N. Potter, 1989.

— and Liza Prior Lucy. *Glorious Patchwork.* New York: C. N. Potter, 1997.

— and Liza Prior Lucy. *Passionate Patchwork.* New York: C. N. Potter, 2001.

Gibson-Roberts, Priscilla. *Ethnic Socks and Stockings: A Compendium of Eastern Technique and Design.* Sioux Falls,

S. Dak.: XRX Books, 1995.

— *Knitting in the Old Way.* Loveland, Colo.: Interweave Press, 1985.

Gottfridsson, Inger, and Ingrid Gottfridsson. *The Mitten Book.* Asheville, N.C.: Lark Books, 1987.

Harrell, Betsy. *Anatolian Knitting Designs: Sivas Stocking Patterns.* Istanbul: Redhouse Press, 1981.

Heathman, Margaret. *Knitting Languages.* Pittsville, Wisc.: Schoolhouse Press, 1996.

Kagan, Sasha. *The Sasha Kagan Sweater Book.* London: Dorling Kindersley, 1984.

— *Sasha Kagan's Big and Little Sweaters.* London: Dorling Kindersley, 1987.

— *Sasha Kagan's Country Inspiration: Knitwear for All Seasons.* Newtown, Conn.: Taunton Press, 2000.

Keele, Wendy. *Poems of Color: Knitting in the Bohus Tradition.* Loveland, Colo.: Interweave Press, 1995.

Khmeleva, Galina. *Gossamer Webs: The History and Techniques of Orenburg Lace Shawls.* Loveland, Colo.: Interweave Press, 1998.

Kolstad, Lise, and Tone Takle. *Small Sweaters: Colorful Knits for Kids.* Loveland, Colo.: Interweave Press, 1995.

— *Sweaters: 28 Contemporary Designs in the Norwegian Tradition.* Loveland, Colo.: Interweave Press, 1992.

Larcom, Lucy. *Poems.* Boston: Fields, Osgood, & Co., 1869.

Lavold, Elsebeth. *Viking Patterns for Knitting: Inspiration and Projects for Today's Knitter.* North Pomfret, Vt.: Trafalgar, 2000.

LeCount, Cynthia Gravelle. *Andean Folk Knitting: Traditions and Techniques from Peru and Bolivia.* St. Paul, Minn.: Dos Tejedoras, 1993.

Lewandowski, Marcia. *Folk Mittens: Techniques and Patterns for Handknitted Mittens.* Loveland, Colo.: Interweave Press, 1997.

Ligon, Linda, ed. *Homespun, Handknit: Caps, Socks, Mittens, and Gloves.* Loveland, Colo.: Interweave Press, 1987.

Lind, Vibeke: *Knitting in the Nordic Tradition.* Asheville, N.C.: Lark Books, 1984.

Melville, Sally. *Sally Melville Styles.* Sioux Falls, S. Dak.: XRX Books, 1998.

Oberle, Cheryl. *Folk Shawls: 25 Knitting Patterns and Tales from Around the World.* Loveland, Colo.: Interweave Press, 2000.

Penders, Mary Coyne. *Color and Cloth: The Quiltmaker's Ultimate Workbook.* San Francisco: Quilt Digest Press, 1989.

Rich, Adrienne. *The Fact of a Doorframe: Poems Selected and New, 1950–1984.* New York: W. W. Norton, 1984.

Righetti, Maggie. *Knitting in Plain English.* New York: St. Martin's Press, 1986.

— *Sweater Design in Plain English.* New York: St. Martin's Press, 1990.

Schulz, Horst. *Patchwork Knitting.* East London, South Africa: Saprotex International, 2000.

— *New Patchwork Knitting: Fashion for Children.* East London, South Africa: Saprotex International, 2000.

Schurch, Charlene. *Mostly Mittens: Traditional Knitting Patterns from Russia's Komi People.* Asheville, N.C.: Lark Books, 1998.

Starmore, Alice. *Aran Knitting.* Loveland, Colo.: Interweave Press, 1997.

— *Book of Fair Isle Knitting.* Newtown, Conn.: Taunton Press, 1988.

— *Fishermen's Sweaters: 20 Exclusive Knitwear Designs for All Generations.* North Pomfret, Vt.: Trafalgar, 1993.

Thomas, Mary. *Mary Thomas's Knitting Book.* New York: Dover, 1972.

Upitis, Lizbeth. *Latvian Mittens: Traditional Designs and*

Techniques. St. Paul, Minn.: Dos Tejedoras, 1981.

van der Klift-Tellegen, Henriette C. *Knitting from the Netherlands: Traditional Dutch Fishermen's Sweaters.* Asheville, N.C.: Lark Books, 1985.

Woolf, Virginia. *To the Lighthouse.* London: Harcourt, 1927.

Zilboorg, Anna. *Fancy Feet: Traditional Knitting Patterns of Turkey.* Asheville, N.C.: Lark Books, 1994.

— *Forty-Five Fine & Fanciful Hats to Knit: Berets, Toques, Cones, Stars, Pentagons, and More.* Asheville, N.C.: Lark Books, 1997.

— *Magnificent Mittens.* Sioux Falls, S. Dak.: XRX Books, 1998.

Zimmerman, Elizabeth. *Knitting Workshop.* Pittsville, Wisc.: Schoolhouse Press, 1981.